THE MISSION

INSIDE THE CHURCH OF JESUS CHRIST OF LATTER-DAY SAINTS

THE MISSION

INSIDE THE CHURCH OF JESUS CHRIST OF LATTER-DAY SAINTS

Introduction by
PRESIDENT GORDON B. HINCKLEY

Epilogue by
ROGER ROSENBLATT

Created and Produced by
MATTHEW NAYTHONS

Director of Photography
ACEY HARPER

EPICENTER COMMUNICATIONS

WARNER BOOKS

A TIME WARNER COMPANY

Created and produced by
Epicenter Communications
Sausalito, CA 94965

Epicenter Communications:

President
Matthew Naythons

Vice President, Managing Editor
Dawn Sheggeby

Vice President, Art Director
Alex Castro

Manager, Photographic Production
Peter Goggin

Editorial Assistants
Kate Warne
Katherine Withers

Director of Photography
Acey Harper

Assistants to the Director of Photography
Shonquis Moreno
Susan Tolleson

Photo Editors
Sandra Eisert
Kathleen Hennessey
Larry Nighswander
George Wedding

Design Consultant
Adrian Pulfer

Editor
Katherine Ball Ross

Captions
Joseph Walker

Creative Consultant
Gordon Bowen

Copy Editor
Lisa Bornstein

Proofreader
Jim Miller

Literary Agent
Deborah Schneider, *Gelfman Schneider*
    Literary Agents

Legal Advisors
Marc Bailin, Esq.
Douglas Ferguson, Esq.

Warner Books, Inc.
1271 Avenue of the Americas
New York, NY 10020

WARNER BOOKS
A Time Warner Company

Printed in Italy
First printing: October 1995
10 9 8 7 6 5 4 3 2

ISBN: 0-446-51889-1
LC: 95-60963

Previous page: The Salt Lake City temple at sunset.
Photograph: Dagmar Fabricius and Randy Taylor

THE MISSION

INSIDE THE CHURCH OF JESUS CHRIST OF LATTER-DAY SAINTS

Why Am I a Member of The Church of Jesus Christ of Latter-day Saints?

by GORDON B. HINCKLEY
President, The Church of Jesus Christ of Latter-day Saints

Why am I a member of The Church of Jesus Christ of Latter-day Saints? The answer, at first blush, is simple. It was the faith of my parents and grandparents. My grandfather was a pioneer in the truest sense. He crossed the plains by ox team and wagon and was a prominent local Church leader. My father was an educator, a businessman, and also a prominent local Church officer.

But my faith is more than a matter of inheritance. Much more. True faith is the fruit of reading and of thinking and of searching prayer. Because it involves a system of belief that is demanding and challenging, true faith has never come easy. Neither has a willingness to try to live the words of Jesus in a society that so often offers only lip service to His teachings.

Why am I a member? Let me briefly suggest some of the beliefs that underlie my love, and that of millions of other men and women, for this vibrant and vital Church and its doctrines.

I believe that there is something wonderfully reassuring about a cause that has endured every conceivable kind of persecution, a cause whose history is told in the steadfastness and courage of its members in the face of withering adversity.

More than 6,000 of our people lie buried on the long trail that led from the Mississippi River and the fair city of Nauvoo, Illinois, to the valley of the Great Salt Lake. My grandfather set out with his young wife for the valleys of the West. She died along the way. With his own hands he dug a shallow grave, fashioned a crude coffin from wood of his own cutting, and left behind a hallowed, lonely burial place, the location of which none of us knows. For the remainder of that long journey, he carried in his arms his motherless infant.

My wife's grandmother was a young woman of 12 when she left England with her family in 1856. They were late in getting started along the pioneer trail. Over 200 of their companions died in the snow-laden storms that whipped across the highlands of what is now Wyoming. Her brother died.

View from atop the Salt Lake City Temple.
Photograph: Thomas Epting

1

Her baby sister died. And before they reached the end of that terrible journey, her mother died. Her own feet were frozen. Using the only tools available—a butcher knife and a meat saw—the doctor amputated her toes. For the remainder of her life, she walked in pain.

One cannot look back to forebears of this kind without a deep introspective probing, without asking the question, Why did they do it? The answer comes: it was because of the conviction they carried in their hearts. It was because the religion they believed in was greater than wealth or security or ease of living; it was more precious than life itself. Their faith was the work of God, worthy of any sacrifice.

I believe in the doctrine that answers the eternal questions, Where did I come from? Why am I here? Where am I going? The theology of this Church teaches that all men and women are sons and daughters of God, that we lived with Him in a premortal state, and that the lives we live today are part of a great eternal journey. We have been endowed with divine qualities and instincts, and we have been sent here "for a wise and glorious purpose." Our earthly state is a season of testing and opportunity. It is a period in which to prepare for the next life. Immortality is as certain as mortality.

I believe in a religion that unequivocally affirms the divinity of the Lord Jesus Christ. Along with other Christians, we accept the Holy Bible as containing the word of God. The Old Testament holds a special place in our theology. The New Testament becomes a declaration of the earthly mission of the promised Messiah, whom we accept and proclaim as Savior and Redeemer. The Lord said, "In the mouth of two or three witnesses every word may be established" (Matthew 18:16). The Bible is the testament of the Old World. The Book of Mormon stands as another witness of Jesus Christ— it is the testament of the New World. Its power for good has been demonstrated again and again. Millions over the earth who have read it and prayed over its truth have borne witness in their hearts to its divine origin and to its power to change lives.

I believe in a religion that teaches the reality and importance of continuous revelation. I have difficulty with the philosophy that God revealed His will to prophets in ancient days when life was relatively simple but that His mouth is closed in these complex and difficult times. We need revelation today as much as it was needed at any point in the history of the earth.

Today, as in times past, the Church is led by the spirit of revelation. We sustain a group of three men in the First Presidency and another twelve men in the Quorum of the Twelve Apostles as "prophets, seers, and revelators." I have seen the power of revelation manifested among them.

I believe in a faith that is a constant in a world of shifting values. We have seen a tremendous change in patterns of moral and spiritual conduct in the last few years. Churches are the great conservators of truth. My religion continues to teach, without equivocation or apology, that personal virtue is to be cherished, that honesty and integrity are central to our conduct, that civility is to be practiced, that kindness is an incumbent responsibility, and that respect for the beliefs and practices of others is a principle that cannot be avoided if one is a Christian. We can disagree with others on matters of doctrine without becoming belligerent. An article of our faith states: "We claim the privilege of worshipping Almighty God according to the dictates of our own conscience, and allow all men the same privilege, let them worship how, where, or what they may" (Article of Faith 11).

I believe in a religion that offers opportunity for growth, training, education, and progress. Wherever it is established, its great work of administration is carried by those who come from the rank and file of the membership. No matter where the Church goes, one of its first responsibilities is to train leaders. Local officers of the Church in Japan are Japanese. Those in Norway are Norwegians. Every man who lives a life in harmony with the standards of the Church is ordained to the priesthood—it is not a privilege reserved for a select few. There are literally hundreds of thousands of local officials, who serve without compensation out of a love for the Lord and for all people for whom they are given responsibility. While performing such unselfish service, these individuals develop skills of leadership and habits of work that benefit them in their regular employment.

Because the Church has no paid local clergy, it has the means to construct the buildings it needs and to carry on many other programs that enrich the lives of its members.

I believe in a religion that honors and respects womanhood. We declare without equivocation that in this Church a woman walks neither ahead of her husband nor behind him but at his side as his equal. Women are afforded challenging opportunities for leadership, for teaching, for growth and education of the mind and heart. Women give doctrinal sermons in the sacrament meetings of the Church. They operate the oldest continuous organization for women in the world—and perhaps the largest as well, with more than 3 million members. In more than 150 nations, Mormon women carry on extensive programs in fostering education, spiritual development, and service to others.

I believe in a religion that offers to every individual the right to know for himself or herself whether it is true. Jesus said, "If any man will do his will, he shall know of the doctrine, whether it be of God, or [whether] I speak of myself" (John 7:17).

The strength of the Church lies not in its physical assets but rather in the hearts of its people. The first Sunday of each month, all members are urged to go without two meals and to give the equivalent value for the care of the poor. No one suffers in this process. Any of us with a little self-discipline can practice this simple regimen. And out of this practice come the funds, substantial in number, to meet the needs of those in distress. While governments wrestle with complex and costly welfare programs, the Church endeavors to take care of its own. This program has resulted in the blessing of uncounted numbers of men and women in various parts of the world, members of the Church as well as nonmembers, who have found themselves destitute in circumstances beyond their control.

Being a Latter-day Saint involves the sacrifice of time and means. It entails the consecration of effort and the patterning of one's life in harmony with the gospel of Jesus Christ. But all of this brings satisfaction, fulfillment, peace of mind—an actual experience of happiness—as people reach out to serve one another.

I believe in a Church whose teachings are lofty, uplifting, and inspiring. Note the following doctrinal declarations:

"The glory of God is intelligence."

"Whatever principle of intelligence we attain unto in this life, it will rise with us in the resurrection. And if a person gains more knowledge and intelligence in this life through his diligence and obedience than another, he will have so much the advantage in the world to come."

"We believe in being honest, true, chaste, benevolent, virtuous, and in doing good to all men. . . . If there is anything virtuous, lovely, or of good report or praiseworthy, we seek after these things."

To return to my original question, Why am I a member of The Church of Jesus Christ of Latter-day Saints? I have given you a few of many reasons. I could name others. They are all of tremendous consequence to me. They are of similar consequence to millions of other men and women around the world.

I invite you to open the pages of this remarkable book and to look into the lives of our people. They speak many languages and live in a variety of societies all over the world. And each of them can stand and say, as I say: This religion is true. It is the work of God. It is the way to happiness in this life and eternal progress in the life to come.

LDS members of the humanitarian aid group Choice survey the Sierra de los Huicholes mountains from a ridge above their campsite in Las Guayabas, Mexico.
Photograph: Robin Bowman

Major Events in the History of The Church of Jesus Christ of Latter-day Saints

• **Early spring, 1820, near what is now Manchester, New York**
Fourteen-year-old Joseph Smith announces that God the Father and Jesus Christ appeared to him in a grove of trees near his home in upstate New York—an event called "The First Vision"—in answer to his prayers to know which church to join.

• **September 22, 1827, near Manchester, New York**
According to Church teachings, an angelic vistor named Moroni delivers to Joseph Smith the gold plates upon which are written a scriptural record that will be translated and published three years later as the Book of Mormon. The scriptures were named for a prophet believed to have lived on the North American continent in ancient times.

• **May, 1829, Harmony, Pennsylvania**
Mormons believe that John the Baptist and then the apostles Peter, James, and John appeared to Joseph Smith and his scribe Oliver Cowdery and restored the priesthood authority that had been taken from the earth soon after the death of Jesus Christ.

• **April 6, 1830, Fayette, New York**
The Church of Jesus Christ of Latter-day Saints is organized. *(Membership: 6)*

• **February 14, 1835, Kirtland, Ohio**
The ecclesiastical structure of the Church begins to take shape as the Quorum of the Twelve Apostles is organized and its members are sent into the world to preach the gospel. *(Membership: 4,372)*

• **March 27, 1836, Kirtland, Ohio**
Joseph Smith, the Church's first president, dedicates the first LDS temple, the Kirtland Temple. *(Membership: 13,292)*

• **July 19, 1837, Great Britain**
Heber C. Kimball and Orson Hyde arrive in the British Isles, the first LDS missionaries to venture beyond North America. *(Membership: 16,282)*

• **March 17, 1842, Nauvoo, Illinois**
Joseph Smith organizes the Female Relief Society of Nauvoo, later known as the Relief Society, and charges its members with the responsibility of caring for the poor and the sick. *(Membership: 20,856)*

• **June 27, 1844, Carthage, Illinois**
An angry mob attacks and kills Joseph Smith and his brother, Hyrum, while they are imprisoned at Carthage. *(Membership: 26,146)*

• **July 24, 1847, Utah**
Brigham Young, the Church's second president, arrives with his advance pioneer company in the Valley of the Great Salt Lake, where the Church will finally make its home and establish its headquarters. *(Membership: 34,694)*

• **January 3, 1876, Provo, Utah**
Brigham Young Academy, later known as Brigham Young University, is founded as an institution teaching secular and religious studies. *(Membership: 107,167)*

• **September 24, 1890, Salt Lake City, Utah**
Wilfred Woodruff, the Church's fourth president, issues The Manifesto, a document that officially discontinues the practice of plural marriage. *(Membership: 188,263)*

• **November 13, 1895, Salt Lake City, Utah**
The Church's genealogical organization is formed as the basis of LDS members' efforts to extend religious ordinances to their "kindred dead." *(Membership: 223,369)*

• **April, 1936, Salt Lake City, Utah**
In response to the Great Depression, the Church introduces a welfare program intended to serve needy members around the world. *(Membership: 750,384)*

• **June 9, 1978, Salt Lake City, Utah**
Spencer W. Kimball, the Church's 12th president, announces the revelation that extends "the blessing of the priesthood to all worthy male members of the Church"—including, for the first time, blacks. *(Membership: 4,166,854)*

• **March 3, 1987, Jerusalem, Israel**
The Brigham Young University Jerusalem Center is opened. *(Membership: 6,275,097)*

• **December 11, 1994, Mexico City, Mexico**
The 2,000th stake of The Church of Jesus Christ of Latter-day Saints is dedicated by Howard Hunter, the Church's 14th president. *(Membership: 9,024,569)*

I

Families Are Forever

What is a family?

Not so long ago that was a simple question, with a simple answer: a family is a father, a mother, brothers, and sisters living together, working together, spending time together, and pulling together in a spirit of love and harmony. With the passage of time, however, and as a result of powerful social and economic conditions, the traditional concept of family has been turned inside out. And more and more, children are being raised in ways that are anything but "traditional."

Today Mormons, like everyone else, are influenced by what goes on in the world. But if statistics are any indication, Mormons tend to respond to real-life pressures by clinging to each other just a little more tenaciously than other families do. The reason? It is probably best summed up by the fact that home and family lie at the very heart of LDS theology. The Church teaches that the family unit is sacred and that it can exist intact forever.

While the Supreme Being is referred to as God, He is most often called Heavenly Father or Our Father in Heaven, and we humans are His spirit children. Jesus Christ, whom Mormons worship and revere, is referred to as Elder Brother as often as He is called Lord or Savior. And when Mormons address each other, there is no Mr. or Mrs. or Miss or Ms.—it's Brother or Sister, spoken with familial love and respect.

Through priesthood ordinances performed in special buildings called temples, husbands and wives are "sealed" to each other "for time and for all eternity." Their children are likewise sealed to them, just as they are sealed to their own parents. The sealing of parents to each other and to their children creates an eternal chain of generations bound for all time by love and faith. It's no wonder, then, that Mormons tend to view heaven as an extension of earthly domestic existence, often referring to the life after this one as a return to their "heavenly home." Nor is it surprising that Latter-day Saints devote considerable time and attention to genealogical work for their "kindred dead." The ordinances of the temple can be performed vicariously on behalf of those who have already passed on, forging ancestral links in an eternal family chain.

All of which has an impact on the way Mormon families get along. Relationships in this life suddenly assume new meaning when their eternal nature is taken into consideration. After all, Mormons are taught that "families are forever." And "forever" is an awfully long time.

Photograph: Joel Sartore

FAITH BEGINS AT HOME

Baptism in Alaska

When Jacob Bodily of Takotna, Alaska, turned eight—"the age of accountability" for Mormons—his family began to plan for his baptism. Because the Bodilys live hundreds of miles from the nearest LDS meetinghouse, it was decided that the ceremony would take place in a nearby beaver pond, *previous page.*

With family and friends watching, Jacob and his father, Lee, a Mormon elder, wade into the pond, *top left.* But when Lee tries to baptize Jacob in the near freezing waters, the boy struggles, *top right,* and the crown of his head is not fully immersed, as required by LDS theology. The boy clings to his father, *above,* and pleads with him not to be submerged again. "I won't make him do it if he doesn't want to," Lee says. Eventually an alternative is suggested, and Jacob is baptized in the family's garage in a taxidermy tub, *right.*

Photographs: Rich Frishman

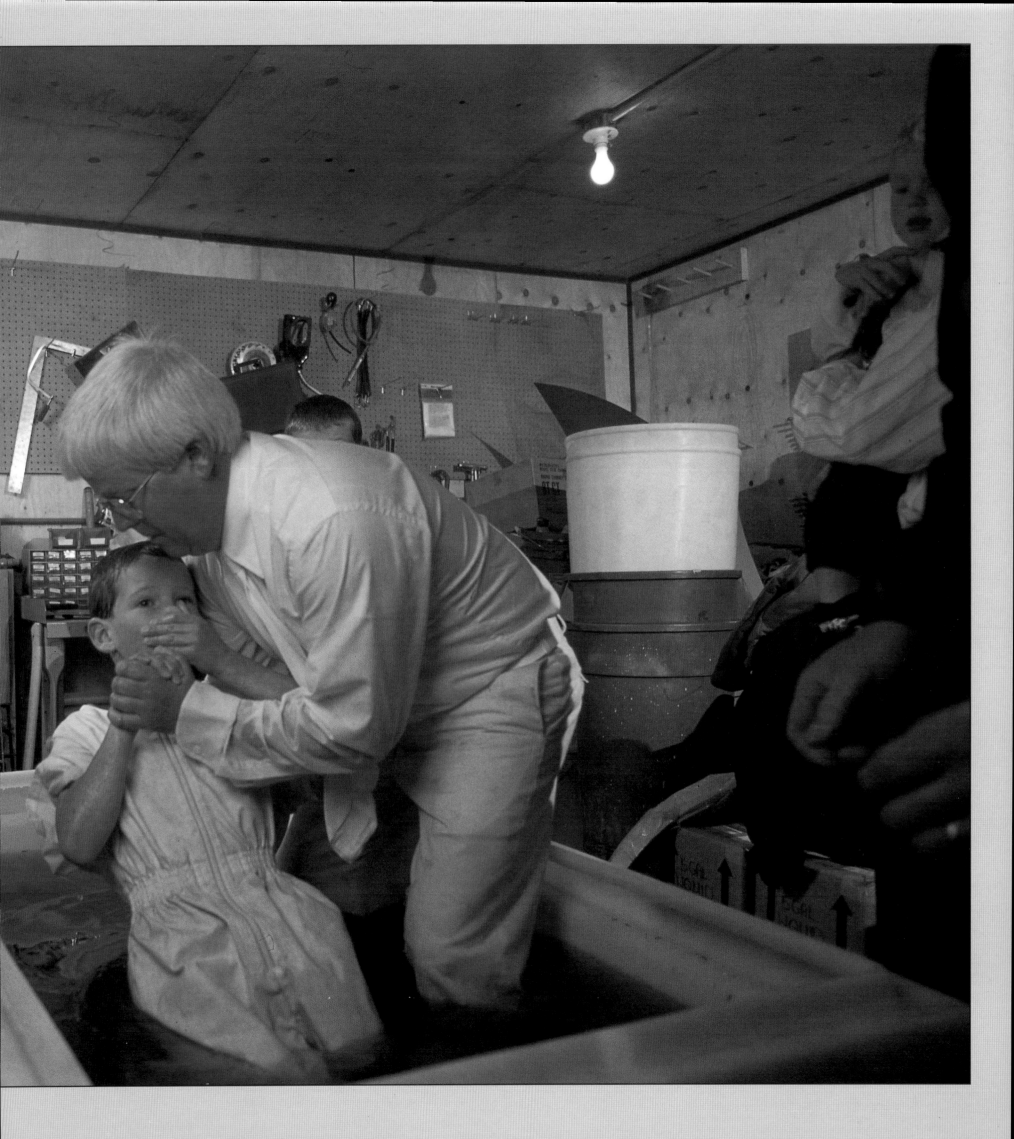

Brian Corbett of Salt Lake City, *above,* takes a break in the midst of Christmas festivities and embraces his seven-month-old daughter, Marli. Since Mormons believe, as one Church leader noted, that "no other success can compensate for failure in the home," activities aimed at strengthening the family are approached with religious zeal and fervor—and not just on special occasions but all year round. One night each week is set aside by faithful Latter-day Saints as "family home evening," when parents and children step away from the cares and challenges of the world to focus their time and attention on each other. For some, it is a time to discuss important issues. For others, it is a time to laugh and pray together. Two-year-old Whitney, *right,* steals the show during family home evening in the home of Elmo and Kathy Robinson of Friendswood, Texas.

Photographs: above, Joel Sartore; right, C. J. Walker (digital manipulation by Impact Media Group)

Sixteen-year-old Brittany Fairclough of Los Angeles, *left*, receives a blessing from her father, Michael, as she prepares to begin a new school year. Such blessings are seen as an extra source of spiritual insight and direction and can be inspiring to parent and child alike. Just prior to receiving a similar pre-school blessing from her father, Mejkin Legler of Springfield, Virginia, *above*, records her feelings and impressions in her journal. Journal keeping, while not a requirement of the faith, is strongly urged as a way of preserving a "personal history" for future generations.

Photographs: left, Jan Sonnenmair; above, Barbara Ries

Personal worship and contemplation are crucial to spiritual development, even for young Latter-day Saints. Eight-year-old Kevin Judson of Springfield, Virginia, *below*, kneels to pray before going to sleep. *Above left,* nine-year-old Cub Scout Garet Legler, also of Springfield, writes about the day's activities in his journal. *Below left,* Garet's older brother, Derrik, describes one of the most significant rites of passage for a Mormon boy—receiving the Aaronic Priesthood—in a special journal his family keeps for important events. "I got the priesthood today," the 12-year-old writes. "It was the greatest feeling of my life. As my Dad ordained me I felt a great feeling of peace, warmth and love."

Photographs: Barbara Ries

Dancing has always been part of the Mormon social culture. Church founder Joseph Smith held numerous balls and dances at the Nauvoo House in Nauvoo, Illinois, and Brigham Young often called for dancing during rest stops along the Mormon pioneer trail. The Gold & Green Ball, once a widely celebrated social event, is now held in only a few places. The one shown here, in Perth, Australia, is more than just a great occasion to wear fancy dancing shoes, like those adorning the feet of Gaye Reeves, *below*. It is a place for the generations to mix in an evening of shared fun. *Above right*, a father enjoys a dance with his teenage daughter. *Below right*, the evening turns livelier when the teenagers start dancing with each other.

Photographs: Tony McDonough

For the Young family of Nevada's Big Smoky Valley region, life is a mix of hard work, lively play, and religious devotion. Three generations of the extended family live together on the Birch Creek Ranch in the heart of central Nevada's ranching and mining district, where they have operated ranching and trucking businesses for 35 years. When the chores are done and the schoolwork is finished, the children enjoy romping together on the family's trampoline, *left*. After dinner, Darrel and Carol Young gather their children around the table to read and discuss the Book of Mormon, *below*. Each family member takes a turn reading from the book and then talking about the relevance of the scripture to daily life.

Photographs: Olivier Laude

Missionary work among Native Americans has been important to Latter-day Saints since the days of Joseph Smith, who taught that many Native Americans are Lamanites, descendants of the ancient Israelites who migrated to the Western Hemisphere around 600 B.C. The Book of Mormon is the story of these people. Members of the tribe's competing clans attend a powwow, *above,* at the Jicarilla Apache Reservation in Dulce, New Mexico. Sister Grob, a Mormon missionary serving on the reservation, visits LDS convert Martha Paiz (left) in her scrub oak lean-to, *below left.* Celvin Young, *above left,* one of Martha's relatives, chops wood during the powwow.

Photographs: Rick Rickman

Young Jason Osumo, *above,* visits his friend, branch president Nicomedes Palomo, at work—a pedicab on the streets of Manila. Palomo catches up on his Book of Mormon reading as Jason keeps a sharp eye out for customers. Close-knit wards can become a kind of extended family for members. In Western Samoa, a boy dives into a pool during a family outing in the Sauniatu Valley, *near right,* and the Elia Tufuga family gathers for family home evening, *far right.*

Photographs: above, Paul Chesley; right, Ed Kashi

"On family home evening, it doesn't really matter what you do," one LDS father observed. "The only thing that matters is being together. And being loved." That is especially true for Dave Oreno, an inmate at the Utah State Prison at Draper. For nine years, he has been sharing family home evening with the J. Matthew and Patricia Limburg family of Magna, Utah, in the prison's chapel, *above*. "We aren't related," Oreno (center) says, "but they're my family." *Right*, the Dipaz family in Lima, Peru, spends part of their family home evening reading to each other by lamplight.

Photographs: above, Joel Sartore; right, Vera Lentz

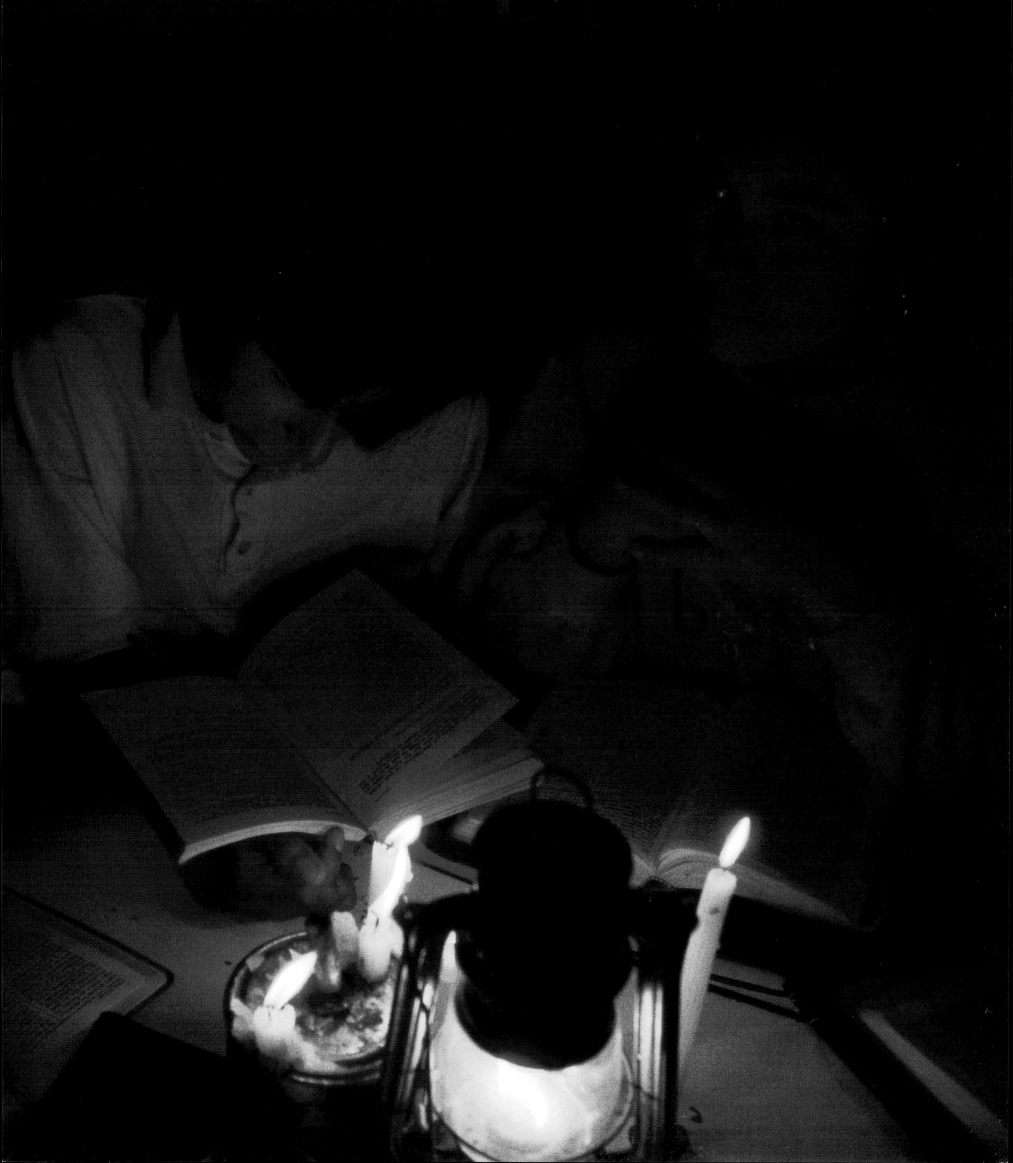

For the few Latter-day Saints living on the islands of New Zealand, opportunities to worship with other Mormons occur rarely. The Ngawaka family of Flat Island uses a boat to travel to Great Barrier Island to meet with other Church members. They also use the boat to reach the makeshift meetinghouse, *above,* at the opposite end of their own island. *Near left,* the family returns from a day spent at the beach together. One of the Ngawaka children, *far left,* stops to play with a neighbor's cattle along the way.

Photographs: Ed Kashi

Ray Close, *left*, known professionally as Ireland's "Stormin' Mormon," unleashes a furious left hook during a workout at a gym in downtown Belfast. *Above*, Ray shows a softer, gentler side as he teaches his seven-year-old son, William, how to pray, while five-year-old Benjamin sits nearby. In 1994, when a brain scan showed a medical problem that threatened to take him out of the ring, he told a newspaper reporter, "I have my family and I have my faith. Those are the things that really matter." He has since been given clearance by the Irish boxing authorities to continue his pursuit of the super-middleweight title.

Photographs: Barry Lewis

In their home in the Dominican Republic, Rosa and Mariano Castillo, *above,* kneel in family prayer with their three children. During family home evening, *below right,* they share stories from the scriptures. The Castillos are part of the growing LDS population in the islands of the Caribbean. The Church has prospered here, despite living conditions that make it difficult to take anything for granted—even something as basic as fresh water, which is carefully transported by a local boy, *above right.*

Photographs: Robin Bowman

Following page: The descendants of Daniel Wood, a Canadian who was converted by Brigham Young, celebrate at a reunion of the extended family near Logan, Utah. Such large-scale family gatherings—this one involves more than 150 people—are common among Latter-day Saints, who believe that "families are forever."

Photograph: Dagmar Fabricius and Randy Taylor

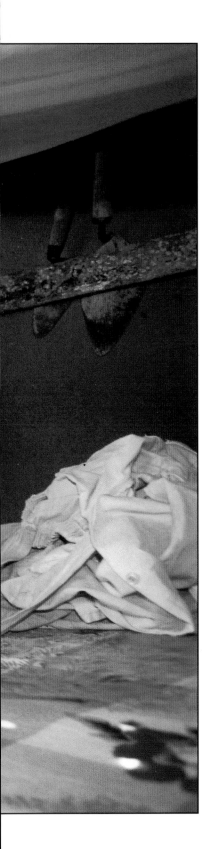

A NEW GENERATION

Following the Pioneers

Young Mormons and their youth leaders from Arvada, Colorado, participate in a Pioneer Trek, *previous page,* during which they reenact the experiences of their pioneer forebears, whose courage in the face of hardship has become the stuff of legends over the past century and a half. Two young men, *above,* survey the encampment of 225 youths and adults who will pull 21 handcarts more than 40 miles along the trail from Casper, Wyoming, to Independence Pass, which was covered by the ill-fated Martin and Willie handcart companies in 1856. More than just an educational activity, the trek is long and difficult, *right,* requiring the best pushing and pulling efforts of the entire group.

Following page: A camp doctor, *above left,* treats blisters on the sore feet of one participant. *Below,* even the rigors of the Pioneer Trek aren't enough to diminish this couple's enthusiasm for an impromptu hoedown near one of the small campfires. A modern-day trekker, *right,* inspects the pioneer names inscribed in Independence Rock, otherwise known as the Register of the Desert, 20 miles south of Casper, Wyoming. The rock was a resting place along the way for virtually all groups traveling on the Oregon and Mormon pioneer trails.

Photographs: Paul Chesley

Annual summer encampments for young women ages 12 to 18, such as this one near Nauvoo, Illinois, *below,* offer a sense of tradition, lots of swimming, *right,* and plenty of time for quiet contemplation and scripture study, *left.* One of the highlights of the camp is the late-night fireside testimony meeting, during which the young women share their most tender emotional and religious feelings in a spirit of love and sisterhood. For girls who live in areas where there are comparatively few Latter-day Saints, the camp provides an opportunity to share beliefs and values with a large group of kindred souls.

Photographs: Keri Pickett

The girls who attended the Nauvoo camp in 1994 will probably never forget the impromptu appearance of Gordon B. Hinckley of the Church's First Presidency, *above*. Less than a year later, Hinckley would become the Church's 15th president. The girls listen attentively, *left*, as the man they would later recognize as God's chosen prophet encourages them to live their lives so they "stand as witnesses of God at all times and in all things, and in all places " (Mosiah 18:9). The Church's long-standing partnership with the Boy Scout movement has resulted in a unique wilderness program called Operation On-Target, *right*. During this event, Scout units from Idaho, Utah, and Arizona climb assigned mountain peaks all along the Wasatch Front—from the U.S.–Canadian border on the north, to Arizona on the south. At dawn, they use signal mirrors to relay messages from one peak to the next, some as far as 55 miles away from each other, linking the boys in an early morning blaze of light and fellowship.

Photographs: above and left, Acey Harper; right, Tim Kelly

Erika Ward, *left*, cuddles her infant daughter, Emerald, while watching her husband play in a Church league basketball game in Sandy, Utah. Participation in such sporting events is a common part of LDS culture. Almost every LDS meetinghouse has a "cultural hall," which tends to look more like a gym, with basketball backboards and volleyball equipment, and most wards sponsor teams in various sports. These athletic activities for teenagers and young adults provide organized opportunities for physical recreation, fellowship, and fun—not to mention a chance to practice good sportsmanship skills. Of course, Church-sponsored activities for young people take into account mind as well as body. At Pesega Elementary, *below*, an LDS-owned school in Apia, Western Samoa, Sione Falefata teaches English to sixth graders.

Photographs: left, Joel Sartore; below, Ed Kashi

Rodeo is a popular sport at the LDS-owned Ricks College in Rexburg, Idaho. Although members of the school's rodeo club have placed high at a number of national competitions, as the trophy belt buckles, *near right*, attest, they are probably a little different from other rodeo riders since they abide by the school's code of conduct that prohibits tobacco, drinking, and profanity. A trick-riding cowgirl, *far right*, a member of an all-female riding group called the Americanas, straddles two saddles and makes it look easy. An intricately braided mane, *above*, shows that at Ricks the horses get their fair share of aesthetic attention.

Photographs: Rick Rickman

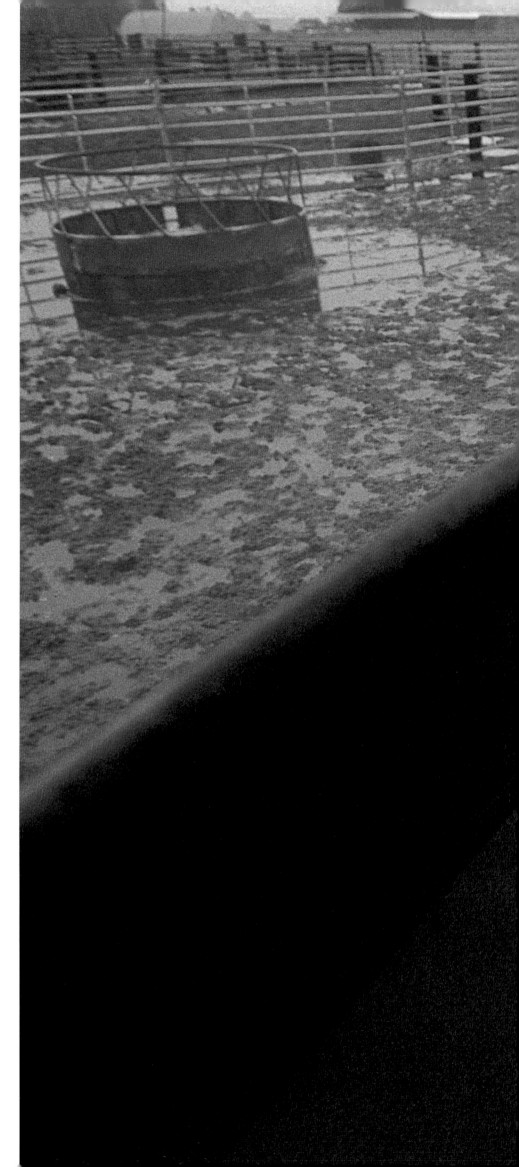

Mel Griffith, *right,* head of the Ricks College Rodeo Club, gets up every morning at dawn to care for the livestock, some of which he personally provides for the program. Approximately 50 head of cattle and 10 horses are used by the rodeo riders each season.

Photographs: Rick Rickman

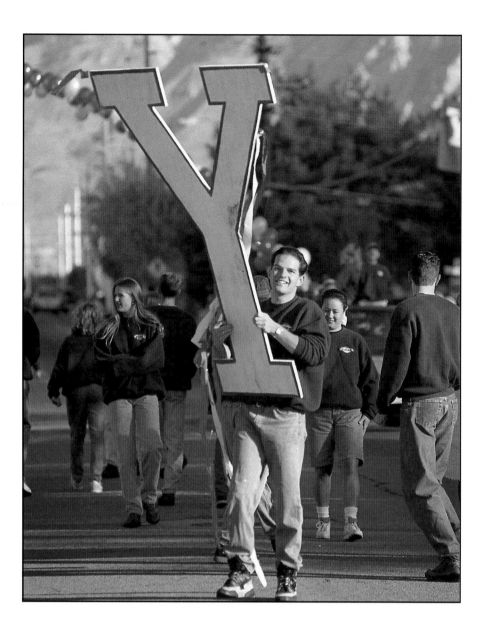

A focal point for religious enthusiasm in the state of Utah is Brigham Young University, the Church's 27,000-student college campus in Provo. Nationally recognized for its academic and athletic programs, BYU is one of the largest private universities in the United States. Campus fervor is never more evident than during Homecoming Week, when alumni arrive from around the world to join students in celebrating the Spirit of the "Y." *Left*, a football fan marches with a big block "Y" in the annual BYU Homecoming Parade near Cougar Stadium. *Right*, dancers enjoy the mood and the music at one of several homecoming balls. *Below*, portraits of past homecoming queens are prominently displayed in the room where the next queen will be crowned.

Photographs: left and right, Rich Frishman; below, Phil Schermeister

In an auditorium at Brigham Young University, *below,* a student grabs a few quiet moments to study. In this place of learning, academic accomplishment is driven by the scriptural philosophy that "the glory of God is intelligence" (Doctrine & Covenants 93:36). *Right,* at Brigham Young University–Hawaii in Laie, Oahu, flags representing the countries of all the current students are interspersed among waving palm trees. The school's academic program focuses particular attention on the students' Asian and Polynesian heritages.

Photographs: right, Robert Holmes; below, Phil Schermeister

The Brigham Young University Jerusalem Center, *below,* gives scholars a firsthand opportunity to explore the relationship between the Mormon Church and ancient Christianity and Judaism from the perspective of LDS theology. The center's massive arches, *left,* provide the framework for a magnificent view of old Jerusalem. Establishing an official LDS presence in Jerusalem has been important to many Mormons who, while Christian by faith, also feel a strong affinity with Judaism. According to Church doctrine, the people of the New World, whose story is told in the Book of Mormon, were Jewish—descendants of the Old Testament's Joseph. Those who accept the Book of Mormon and join the Latter-day Saints become Joseph's descendants "by adoption." In that sense, LDS theology can be viewed as a unique blend of the Old and New Testaments. And where better to pursue these varied interests than in the city where Christianity and Judaism come together?

Photographs: Lori Grinker

Each year hundreds of Latter-day Saints use the Jerusalem Center as headquarters for their tour of historic sites throughout the Holy Land, such as the Wailing Wall in Jerusalem, *right*. These experiences are designed not only to provide students with information but also to enhance their feelings of compassion and tolerance for people of other faith groups. *Below*, Jerusalem Center students pause to pray before embarking upon a field trip to the Great Pyramids near Cairo.

Photographs: Lori Grinker

AN ETERNAL CHAIN

A Young Father's Funeral

Nothing tests faith and family resilience as the unexpected death of a loved one. After Richard Scothern was killed in an avalanche, family, friends, and members of the Ben Lomond Sixth Ward in Utah, *previous page,* rally in support of his young widow, Kari, and his sons, C. J. and Bridger. *Above,* a family photograph is placed on the podium at the front of the Sixth Ward chapel during Richard's funeral service. Following the service, family and friends gather at the Ben Lomond Cemetery, *above right,* where Kari struggles with her emotions as she holds her youngest son, Bridger, on her lap. Meanwhile, three-year-old C. J., *below right,* studies his father's final resting place moments before the casket is lowered into the ground.

Photographs: Joel Sartore

64

Soon after Emmitt Young, *above*, converted to Mormonism, he was diagnosed with a rare and incurable form of cancer and told by his doctors he had only a year and a half to live. Because he was determined to spend his remaining months working for his new Church in whatever way he could, he sought permission to begin his full-time mission early. He began his service in Los Angeles, where he lived, which allowed him to continue medical treatments. The day after the photograph at right was taken, Emmitt died. He was 19 years old.

Photographs: Rick Rickman

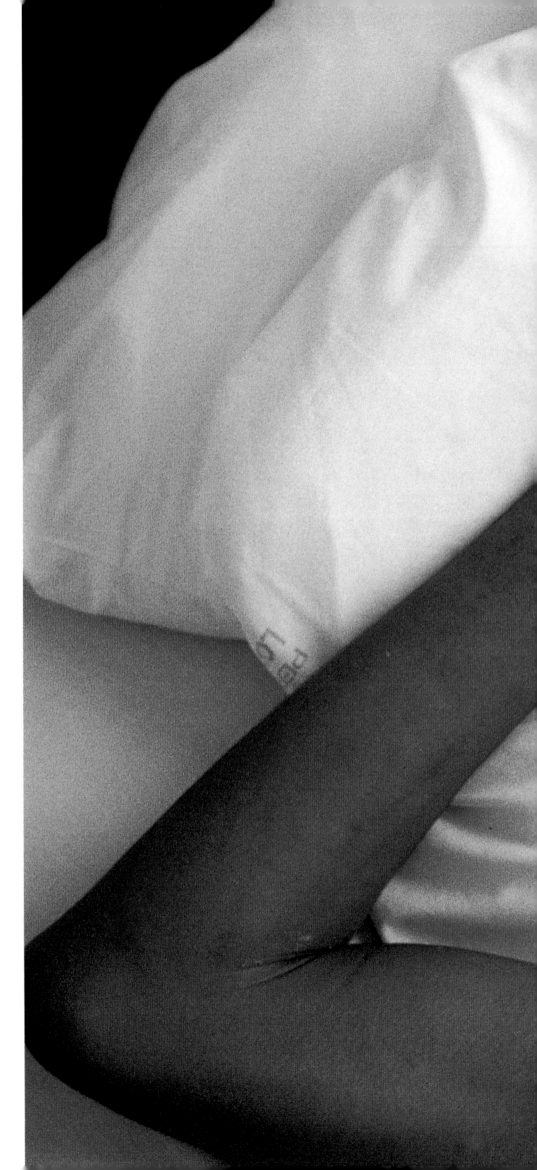

Although he served as the Church's president and prophet for less than nine months, Howard W. Hunter had considerable influence among Latter-day Saints. People responded to his message of love and faithfulness, and whenever he appeared in public, one could sense the tender feelings and high regard in which he was held. When he died in early 1995, mourners stood in long lines to pass by his casket. *Left,* members of the immediate family pay their final respects. *Above right,* Hunter's second wife, Inis (foreground), bows her head during a prayer at her husband's grave site. *Below right,* a father holds his son aloft as the president's casket is wheeled into the Salt Lake Tabernacle for his funeral service.

Photographs: Acey Harper

Donna Jordon, *above,* sits at the reception desk in the Family History Center in Salt Lake City. Behind her, a huge mural depicts the philosophical underpinnings of Mormon genealogical efforts. Care for historical family materials is typical among Mormons, whose beliefs focus on the eternal family unit and religious ordinances that extend throughout time and eternity. The Church compiles huge amounts of genealogical material and devotes entire libraries, like this one at Brigham Young University, *far right,* so that members as well as nonmembers can research their family histories. *Near right,* the displays at the funeral of Paul Kauali'i Parker, an LDS pioneer in Hawaii, provide a time capsule of Hawaiian and Church history.

Photographs: above, Joel Sartore; near right, Robert Holmes; far right, Phil Schermeister

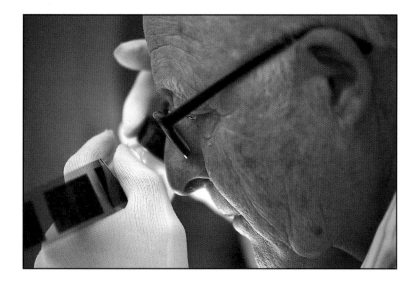

Much of the Church's vast genealogical holdings is stored at the Granite Mountain Vault, *right*, a huge facility carved out of a solid stone mountain just east of Salt Lake City. Under tight security and careful environmental controls, precious documents are preserved and studied, and the genealogical data they contain are extracted. In most cases, the original documents are photographed and transferred to microfilm; *top and above*, staff members retrieve and copy documents from the microfilm, which are then made available to family historians around the country for their genealogical research.

Photographs: right, Matthew Naythons; top and above, Acey Harper

A Scoutmaster, *left,* helps one of his Scouts explore computer-aided genealogy at the FamilySearch Center, located in the Joseph Smith Building in the heart of downtown Salt Lake City. The FamilySearch computer system provides access to the Church's Ancestral File, a genealogical database that compiles names according to family relationships. FamilySearch also makes available the International Genealogical Index (IGI) and other essential information from the Church's vast genealogical holdings. *Above,* a member of a data-collection project in Vancouver, British Columbia, gathers genealogical information at one of the oldest cemeteries in the province. For Latter-day Saints, such efforts on behalf of their "kindred dead" are a literal fulfillment of the prophet Malachi's vision regarding the turning "of the heart of the fathers to the children, and the heart of the children to their fathers" (Malachi 4:6), which is to occur "before the coming of the great and dreadful day of the Lord" (Malachi 4:5).

Photographs: left, Joel Sartore; above, Drew Perine

In Finland, it is traditional to pay tribute to deceased family members by placing candles on their gravestones on Christmas Eve. Integrating this Finnish custom into their Mormon beliefs, members of the Forsman family, *right,* enact the custom in a historic Christian cemetery in Espoo.

Photograph: Jonathan Olley

II

A New Church for a New Land

Although LDS worship services are held on Sundays, membership in The Church of Jesus Christ of Latter-day Saints is not a Sunday-only thing. It is a way of life that affects almost every aspect of existence, requiring energy and commitment every day of the week. In addition to daily prayer and scripture study, both individually and as families, there are weekday activities and events with others in the congregation. For lay leaders, there is the additional responsibility of giving time to those whom they are called upon to serve.

What else do Mormons do to practice their faith? They give ten percent of their income to the Church. They fast the first Sunday of each month and donate to the poor the money they would have spent on food. They don't smoke; they don't drink coffee, tea, or alcoholic beverages; their young people are encouraged not to date until they are 16; and their leaders strongly urge them to avoid entertainment that is obscene, violent, profane, vulgar, or immoral. According to the Church's Articles of Faith: "We believe in being honest, true, chaste, benevolent, virtuous and in doing good to all men.... If there is anything virtuous, lovely, or of good report or praiseworthy, we seek after these things."

Primarily, however, the Church teaches principles, derived from the gospel, that serve as a guide for living and as a source of inner peace and happiness. Following those principles puts people in touch with a Higher Power, which leads to the enriching understanding that God loves them individually and collectively and that He cares for them despite the trials of life. And this understanding, Mormons believe, is what gives them the courage to cope with the stresses of daily existence and the spiritual strength they need in times of crisis.

For Latter-day Saints, the Church provides an opportunity to learn and live eternal principles that will ultimately bring joy into life, in this world and the next.

Photograph: Vera Lentz

FOLLOWING THE PROPHETS

"When the Saints Meet . . ."

From its vantage point atop the highest pinnacle of the Salt Lake Temple, a golden statue of the angel Moroni, *previous page,* heralds the start of another General Conference season. On this biannual occasion, Latter-day Saints from all around the world gather at Church headquarters in Salt Lake City to receive instruction and information from their leaders. For some Latter-day Saints, attendance at General Conference in Utah is a once-in-a-lifetime pilgrimage filled with experiences to be cherished. For others, it is a regular part of doing Church business, with a rush of meetings to attend, appointments to keep, and contacts to make. As a result, conference season turns Temple Square into an intriguing mix of Mecca and Wall Street, with long lines of the faithful, *above,* waiting to be seated in the historic Tabernacle. Some conference-goers begin lining up for morning sessions well before sunrise, *right,* in the hope of securing the seats closest to the Church leaders, especially their prophet.

Photographs: previous page, Joel Sartore; above, Acey Harper; right, Ed Kashi

A security guard, *above,* strides across an aisle in the Tabernacle on Temple Square, using a mirror to check underneath the pews in between general conference sessions. He has a lot of ground to cover, as the silver-domed, oval-shaped building has a seating capacity of nearly 6,000. The building's acoustics are unique. When it is empty, *above right,* tour guides like to have visitors stand at the back of the hall while they go up to the front and drop a pin, which can be clearly heard resonating throughout the building. Filled with conference-goers, *below right,* however, it needs a little help from a state-of-the-art sound-amplification system, which includes translation capabilities for non-English speakers.

Photographs: Acey Harper

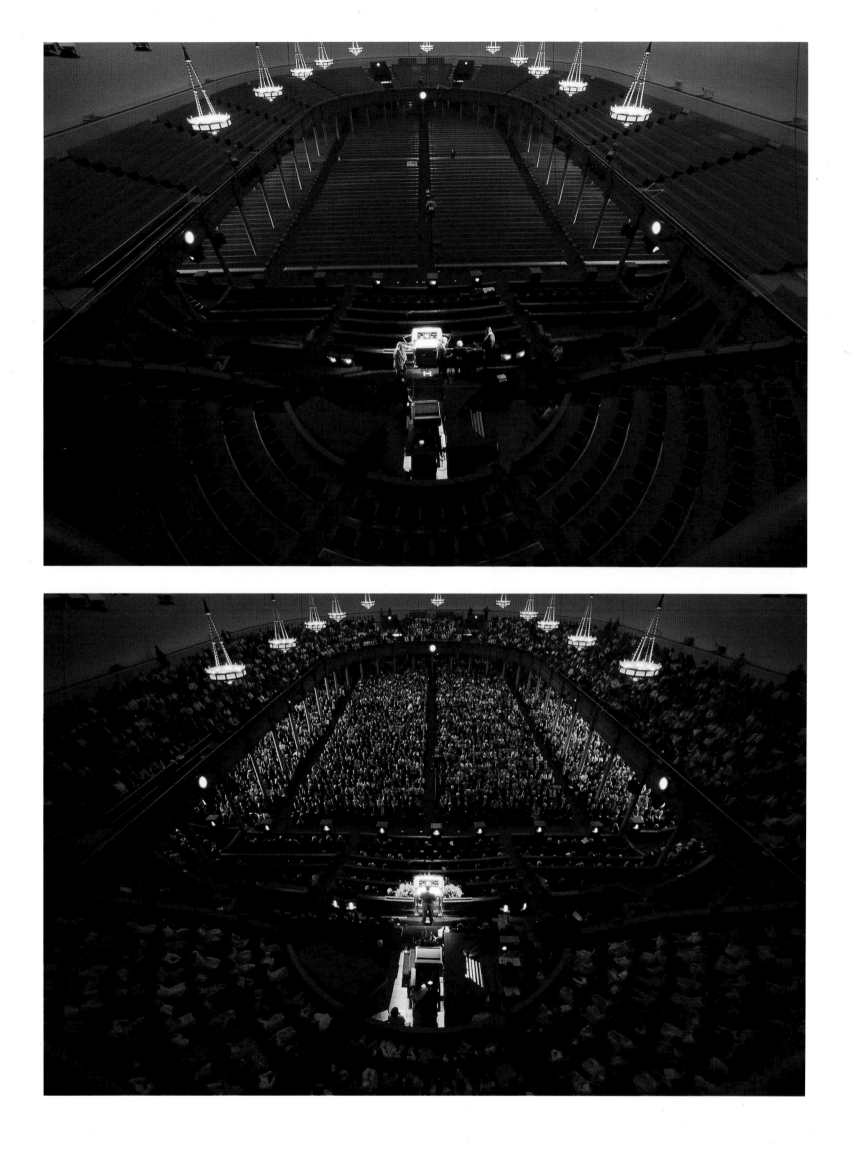

There is a saying in Salt Lake City that "when the Saints meet, the heavens weep," in reference to a curious stormy phenomenon known as "conference weather." But there are no storms on this conference weekend, and the crowds flock to Temple Square on a balmy autumn afternoon, *far right.* Those who are unable to find seats in the Tabernacle simply stroll the square or throw blankets on the lawn, *near right,* soaking up the atmosphere and listening to the sermons of Church authorities via an outdoor public-address system. For many fathers and sons, *above,* attending the conference priesthood session together is a joyful tradition, a bonding time to be savored and enjoyed.

Photographs: above, Acey Harper; near right, Ed Kashi; far right, Mark Philbrick

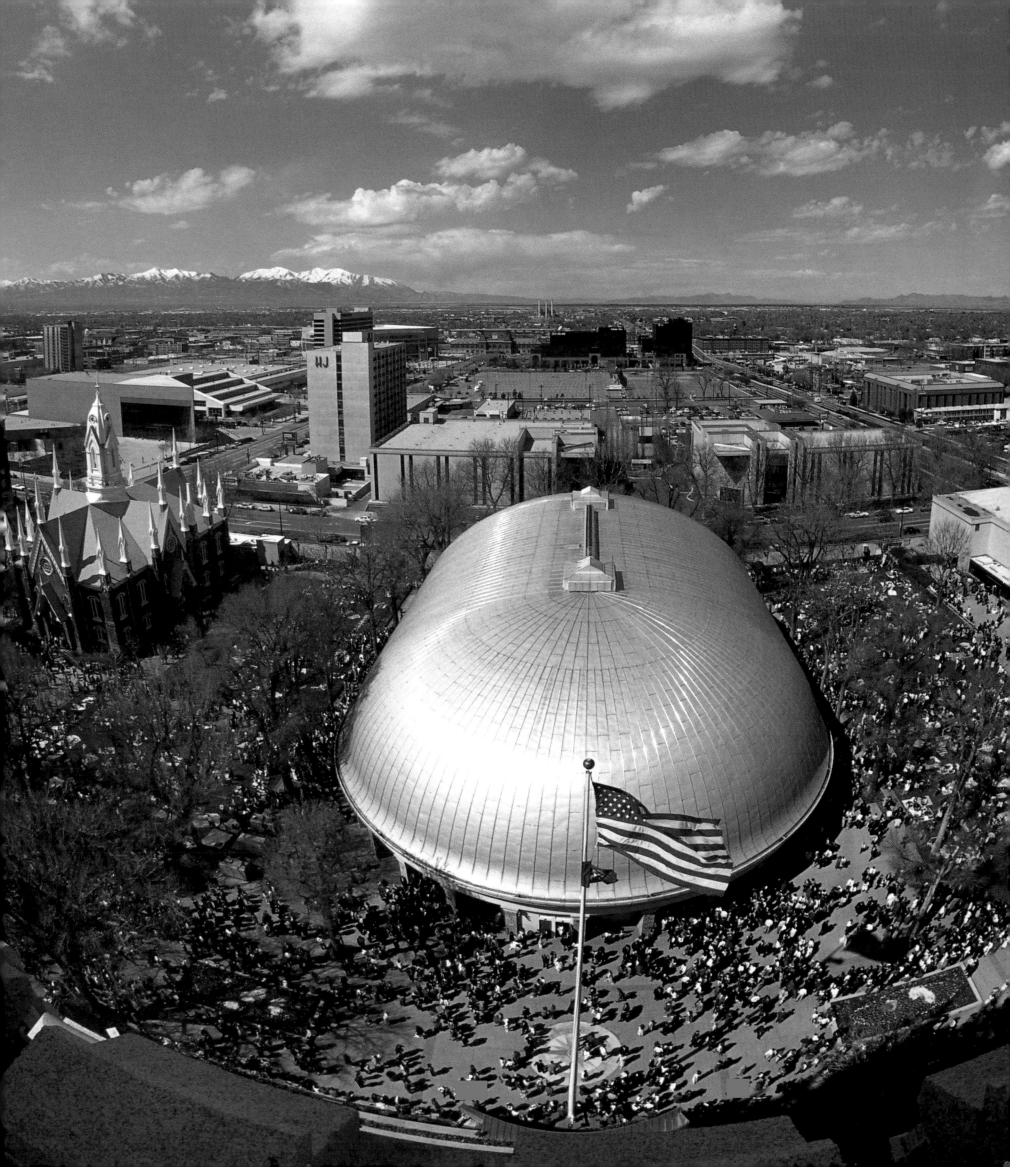

Behind the scenes at General Conference, simultaneous language translation occurs in booths beneath the Tabernacle, *above left.* Translated versions of conference proceedings are available to the audience sitting in the Tabernacle as well as to members around the world, who can view them via satellite transmission or on videotape. Toward the back of the Tabernacle is a sealed off "cry room," *center left,* where parents can take fussy children and still be able to see and hear the conference messages. *Below left,* engineers control everything from lights to podium height to air conditioning in a special control room tucked underneath the Tabernacle balcony. *Below right,* Elaine Jack (left), president of the Relief Society, the Church's organization for women, greets Lorna Hatch (center), a childhood friend from Cardston, Alberta. *Above right,* Elder Dallin H. Oaks (right), a former Utah State Supreme Court justice and now a member of the Church's Quorum of the Twelve Apostles, enjoys a light moment with Elder V. Dallas Merrell of the Second Quorum of Seventy (center) and his cousin, Marlowe D. Merrell (left).

Photographs: Acey Harper

Central to LDS Church governance is the principle of common consent. Members are regularly given the opportunity to raise their right hand to "sustain" their leaders, *right*. While individual policies or programs are not voted upon, a sustaining vote indicates both approval of leaders and a pledge to support them. At this General Conference, there is a new Church president, and so a "solemn assembly" is conducted, during which members stand to sustain him, first in small groups, such as members of the Quorum of the Twelve Apostles, *above*, and then as an entire membership. Even those watching at home on television, like the members of the Kinikini and Vaisa families of West Valley City, Utah, *below*, stand in support of the new prophet.

Photographs: above and right, Acey Harper; below, Ed Kashi

Mormons consider Jesus Christ the head of their Church. The General Authorities, who they regard as Christ's representatives, are the individuals who administer the spiritual and temporal affairs of the Church and its members. The presiding authority of the Church is its president, or prophet, who, with his two counselors, constitute the First Presidency. Next in Church authority is the Quorum of the Twelve Apostles, followed by the Presidency of the Seventy, the First and Second Quorums of the Seventy, and the Presiding Bishopric. The First Presidency and the Quorum of the Twelve Apostles are pictured at right in a rare photograph featuring all 15 members. Seated in front is the First Presidency: the 15th prophet, President Gordon B. Hinckley (center), and his counselors, President Thomas S. Monson (left) and President James E. Faust (right). Standing behind them in order of seniority is the Quorum of the Twelve Apostles (left to right): acting Quorum President Boyd K. Packer and Elders L. Tom Perry, David B. Haight, Neal A. Maxwell, Russell M. Nelson, Dallin H. Oaks, M. Russell Ballard, Joseph B. Wirthlin, Richard G. Scott, Robert D. Hales, Jeffrey R. Holland, and Henry B. Eyring.

Photograph: Acey Harper

Near the home of Joseph Smith in upstate New York, a visitor pauses for reflection in the grove of trees, *right,* where the LDS founder received what Mormons call the First Vision. According to Church doctrine, God and Jesus Christ appeared to the 14-year-old Smith in a miraculous manifestation, which set in motion the process of restoring the gospel. *Above,* President Gordon B. Hinckley (right), the Church's prophet, and Elder M. Russell Ballard of the Quorum of the Twelve Apostles (left) spend a quiet moment in the upstairs room at Carthage, Illinois, where Joseph Smith and his brother, Hyrum, were murdered by an angry mob in 1844.

Photographs: above, Acey Harper; right, Forest McMullin

Mormons believe that, in addition to restoring New Testament Christianity, Church founder Joseph Smith was also charged with integrating new concepts, doctrines, and scriptures, including The Book of Mormon: Another Testament of Jesus Christ. The Hill Cumorah Pageant, *below,* performed annually near Smith's upstate New York home, dramatically portrays the story of the ancient Jews who were led by God to leave Jerusalem and create a new civilization on what is now the American continent. According to Mormon theology, these are the ancestors of many Native American cultures, and the Book of Mormon is the history of their accomplishments, their religion, their wars, and, ultimately, their destruction. The most compelling story of the Book of Mormon, and of the Hill Cumorah Pageant, *right,* occurs when Christ appears to people in the Americas, soon after His death and resurrection.

Photographs: Forest McMullin

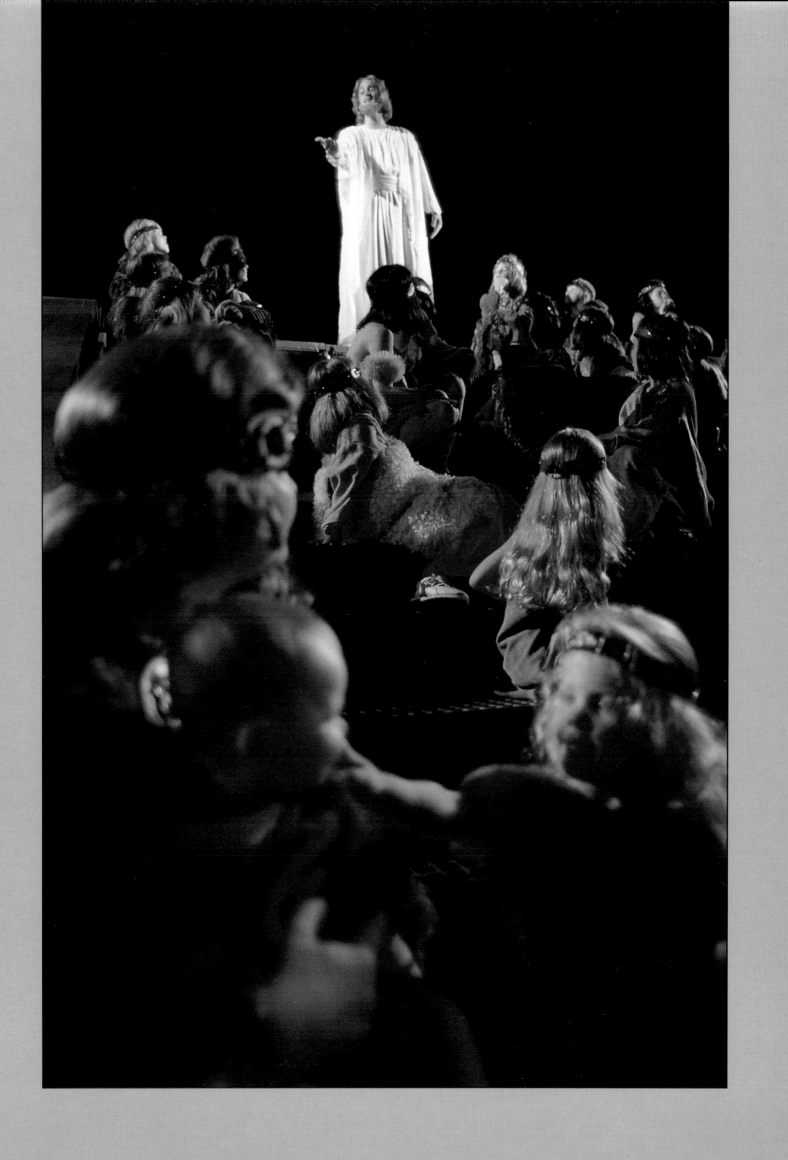

Two girls are dressed in 19th-century costume, *left*, for the Castle Valley Pageant, which celebrates the colonization of the American West by Mormon pioneers. Soon after the murder of Joseph Smith in Illinois, Brigham Young, the Church's second president, led the faithful away from religious persecution in the eastern United States to a place they believed God had chosen for them in the Rocky Mountains. Ever since Young entered the Salt Lake Valley with his first pioneer company on July 24, 1847, and said, "This is the right place," July 24 has been Pioneer Day in Utah, enthusiastically celebrated with parades, rodeos, religious services, and carnivals. *Above*, a sculptured head of Jesus, destined for a Pioneer Day float, is painstakingly carved in a neighborhood garage.

Photographs: Dagmar Fabricius and Randy Taylor

Mormons refer to Joseph Smith, *below left,* as the Prophet of the Restoration. They believe that it was through him that Jesus Christ restored His church and priesthood authority after His mortal ministry had ended. Brigham Young, *above left,* Smith's successor, left an indelible imprint on the Church he led for 33 years, longer than anyone else. But as much as Mormons honor their prophets, they are quick to point out that the real leader of the Church is Jesus Christ, whose presence pervades the Salt Lake City Visitors' Center, *below.*
Photographs: left, Joel Sartore; below, Ed Kashi

Although the Church is international in scope and membership, Salt Lake City is considered its home, if not its birthplace. It is from here that the Church leadership communicates with members all around the world. And it is here that the Church houses its extensive historical and genealogical holdings. Each year, millions of visitors tour Temple Square, where volunteer guides, such as American Chan Young Yi, *left*, and German Patricia Bartsch, *above*, are ready to provide information and to answer questions in a variety of languages.

Photographs: Joel Sartore

For many music lovers, the word "Mormon" is incomplete without the words "Tabernacle" and "Choir." Founded during the Church's Utah pioneer era as a way of bringing culture and refinement to the Mormons' valley home, the Mormon Tabernacle Choir has earned an international reputation for musical excellence through numerous recordings and tours. *Left*, the choir performs its annual Christmas concert in a Tabernacle bedecked with decorations of the season. *Above*, choir members do warm-up exercises in the Tabernacle's basement dressing rooms. *Below*, a technician supplies the live feed for a worldwide television broadcast.

Photographs: Joel Sartore

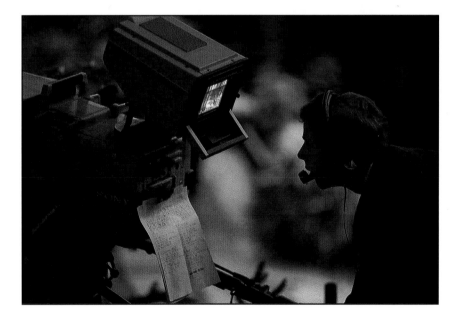

Every Christmas, Temple Square in Salt Lake City is aglow with hundreds of thousands of tiny sparkling lights, *right*. The holiday season is always a festive time of year at the square, attracting thousands of visitors with its multicolored lights, its life-size nativity scene, and musical performances by talented artists from throughout the Mountain West. *Above*, 13-year-olds Kathryn Peterson (left) and Farah Nelson (right) share a joyful moment between holiday events at Temple Square.

Photographs: Joel Sartore

106

A GOOD WAY OF LIFE

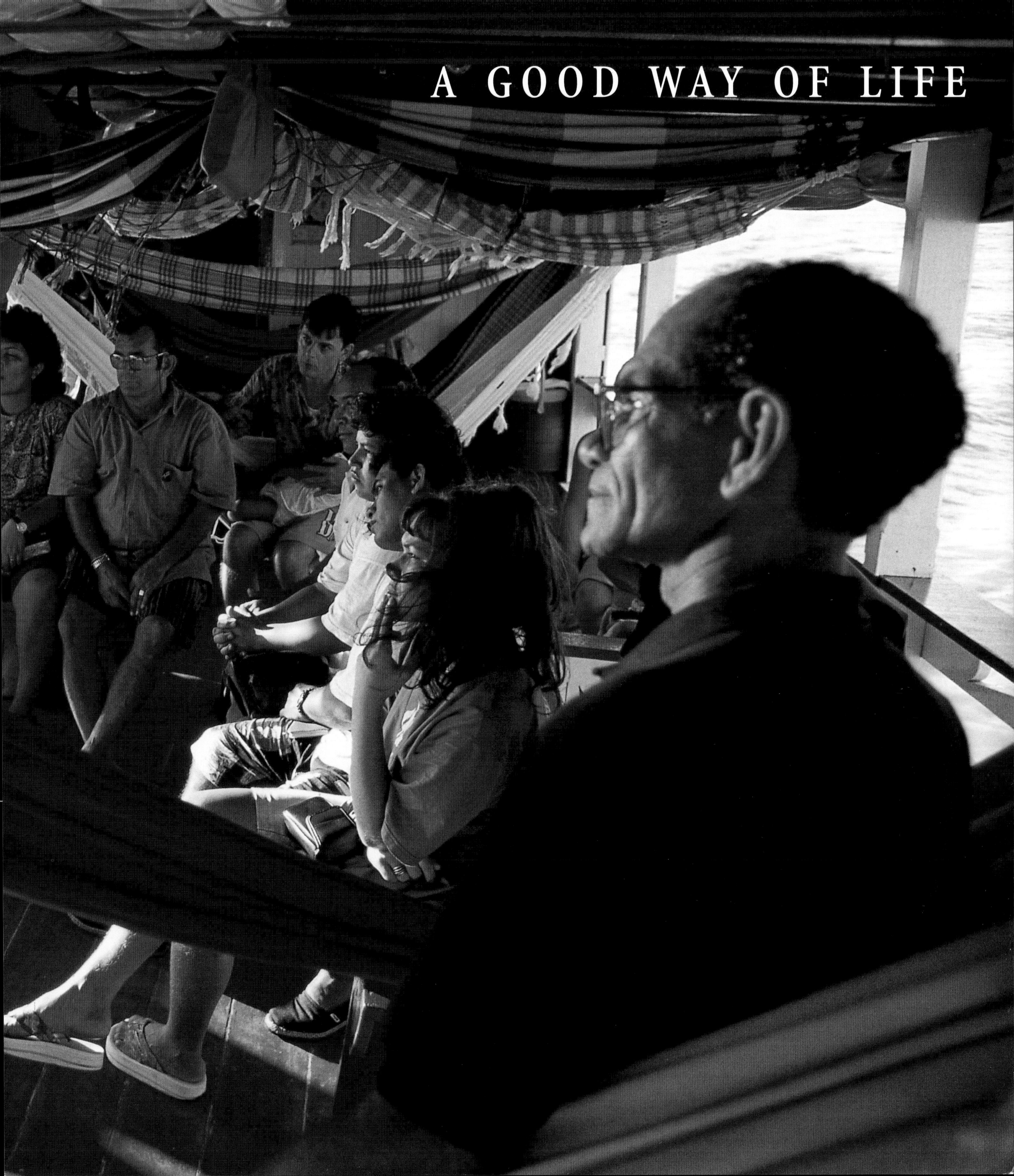

Pilgrimage Down the Amazon

Surrounded by hammocks and driven by faith, *previous page,* a group of 49 Mormons from Manaus, Brazil, launches its annual 12-day, 3,000-mile round-trip pilgrimage to visit the Church's temple in São Paulo, Brazil. It is a journey fraught with difficulty, as the Latter-day Saints must travel in a riverboat down the Amazon, *left,* and the Madeira River. The length of the trip allows plenty of time to study the scripture, *above right,* to rest and relax, *center right* and *below right,* and to prepare spiritually for the highly valued, much-anticipated opportunity of temple worship.

Photographs: Claus Meyer

When the pilgrims aren't searching the shoreline for napping alligators or watching dolphins play alongside the boat, they are apt to be caring for children, *far right,* or preparing meals, *near right,* activities that occupy much of the time on the journey. As the boat travels about 20 miles per hour, the river portion of the trip requires about 72 hours each way. Once the boat docks in Humaitá, two Mormon missionaries greet the travelers, help them disembark, *below,* and board them onto the bus that will take them on the next leg of their journey to São Paulo. There they will visit one of 46 buildings around the world Latter-day Saints consider to be "the House of the Lord."

Photographs: Claus Meyer

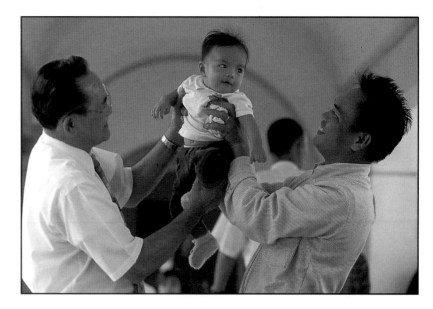

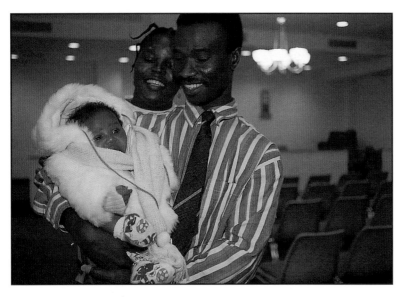

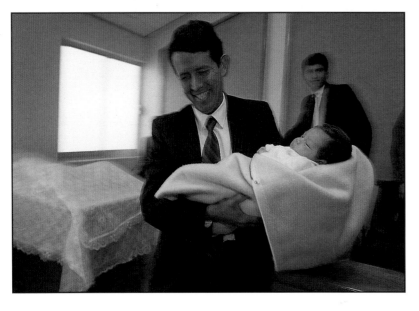

The first Sunday of each month is set aside by Latter-day Saints as a day of fasting and prayer, with the money that would have been spent on food being donated to the Church for the relief of the poor and needy. The focal point of the day is the "fast and testimony meeting," an impromptu worship service during which members stand to share spiritual feelings and experiences. At this meeting, children are brought before the congregation and given a special blessing by their father or other priesthood holders, *right.* Similar to a christening, these blessings are a joyful sacrament for LDS families the world over, whether they are celebrated in, *clockwise from top left,* Moscow, Russia; Manila, Philippines; Detroit, Michigan; Puebla, Mexico; or New York City.

Photographs: clockwise from top left, Nikolai Ignatiev, Paul Chesley, Taro Yamasaki, Robin Bowman, Nina Barnett; right, Robin Bowman

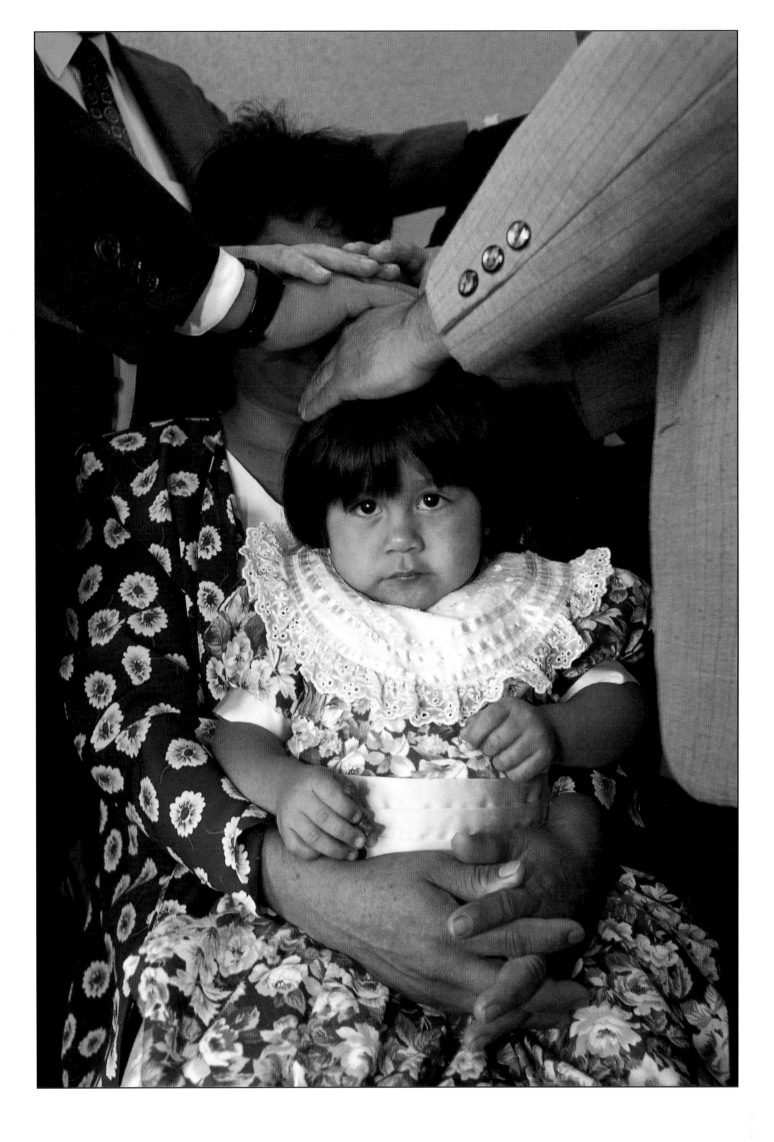

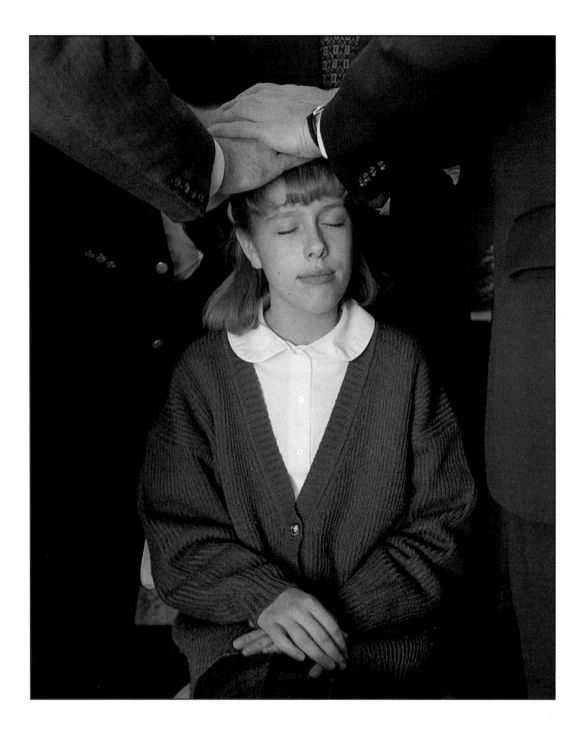

Priesthood authority is a dynamic force in the lives of LDS members. Blessings through the laying on of hands are given regularly and often— at christenings, at confirmations, for healing, during times of difficulty and trial, when new church responsibilities are accepted, and whenever extra spiritual guidance is desired. There is very little form to such blessings; for the most part, the words come through inspiration. And so it is considered important that both the person giving the blessing and the person receiving the blessing be open and receptive to the spiritual promptings of the moment. *Above,* Farah Nelson of Salt Lake City listens carefully as she is "set apart," or invested with authority, to serve as a counselor in the presidency of her class of Beehives, the Church's organization for girls ages 12 and 13. *Right,* a newly baptized convert in Kenya receives a confirmation blessing from LDS missionaries.

Photographs: above, Joel Sartore; right, Lori Grinker

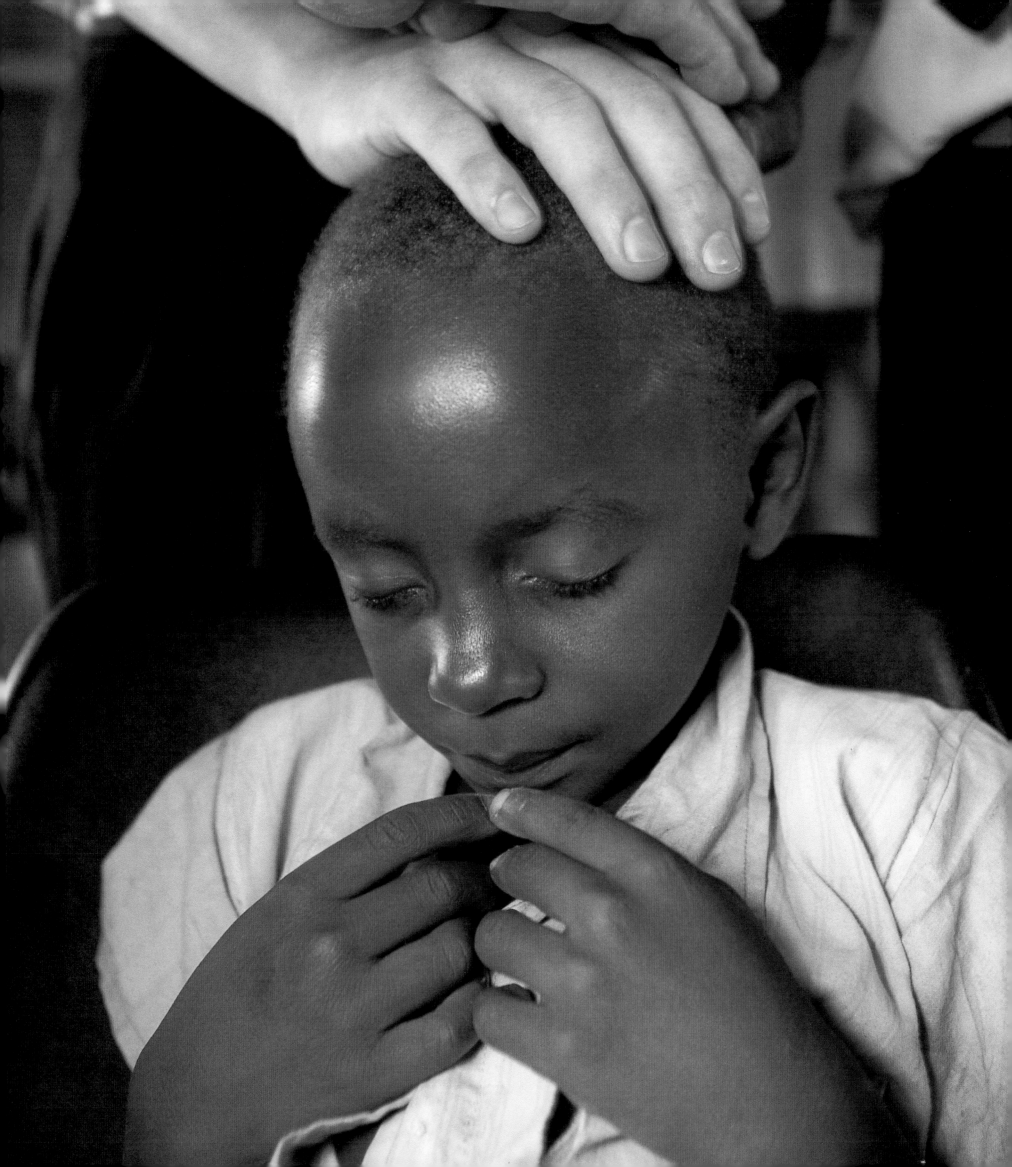

The word "baptism" usually needs to be qualified when talking to LDS members. Baptism, an essential eternal ordinance according to Mormon theology, has at least three different implications. Children who grow up in the Church are baptized at age eight. In Salt Lake City, where the Latter-day Saint population is large, congregational baptismal services for children who reach "the age of accountability" can be crowded and rather lengthy, *near right.* A "convert baptism," such as the baptism of Dr. Robert Attipoe in Orlando, Florida, *far right,* occurs when a mature person chooses to embrace the faith. *Above,* Filipino youths await their turn to perform "baptisms for the dead" in the Church's temple in Manila. Like other temple ordinances, baptisms for the dead are performed by proxies on behalf of ancestors who died before they could be baptized in their lifetime.

Photographs: above, Paul Chesley; near right, Joel Sartore; far right, C. J. Walker

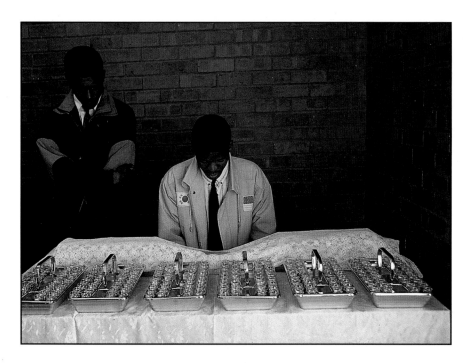

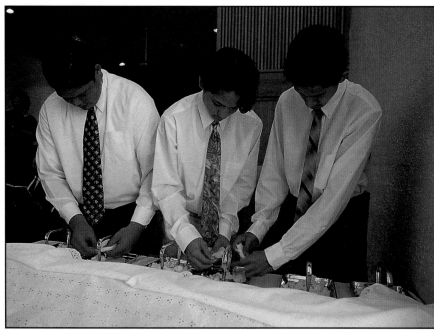

The weekly Sunday worship service in each Mormon congregation is called "sacrament meeting." Its highlight occurs when members partake of the sacrament, or communion, patterned after the Lord's Supper in the New Testament. The LDS sacrament consists of broken bread eaten in remembrance of the body of Christ and tiny cups of water representing His atoning blood. In most congregations, such as in these wards in Kenya, *above left* and *below left,* and in Hawaii, *center left,* young men who hold the priesthood prepare the water and the bread, bless the sacrament, and pass it to the congregation. In an isolated area of New South Wales, Australia, *right,* Stan Hawkins is the only priesthood holder present for a service near an opal mine pit, so he performs the ordinance himself.

Photographs: above left and below left, Lori Grinker; center left, Robert Holmes; right, Emmanuel Santos

Howard McLaughlin serves the sacrament to a resident at a Salt Lake City convalescent center, *right*. Members of McLaughlin's ward regularly provide worship services, entertainment, and blessings of health and comfort to residents of the center, which is located next door to the ward meetinghouse. *Above*, children in the Nottingham Country Ward in Katy, Texas, take the sacrament just before performing as part of the ward's annual "children's sacrament meeting" program. There is no specific age at which children can begin to take the sacrament. Even infants and toddlers eat the bread and drink the water that is served to them, and their parents are encouraged to teach them what the emblems of the sacrament mean. By the age of eight, when they are old enough to be baptized, children are thought to be ready to understand the weekly sacrament service more fully—as an opportunity to renew their baptismal promises, to always remember Jesus Christ, and to live their lives in a Christ-like manner.

Photographs: above, C. J. Walker; right, Joel Sartore

Moses Doug Dipaz, *above,* dressed up in his Sunday best, puts a last-minute shine on his shoes before setting off for church with his mother, Lilia, and two sisters on the hilly outskirts of Lima, Peru, *top.* Today is a special day for the family because the youngest child, Lady Mayra, will be blessed by her father, Bishop Lucio Dipaz. The Dipaz family is typical of Peru's LDS population, in that 60 percent of the country's Mormons are younger than 30 years old. Although Peru remains 90 percent Roman Catholic, Lima claims the second-largest concentration of LDS congregations—after Mexico City—among metropolitan areas outside the United States. *Right,* Jennifer Sosa Soto (right) and her brother Vicente (left) climb a hill outside Lima on their way to religion class in the home of their LDS teacher.

Photographs: Vera Lentz

For active Latter-day Saints, church attendance on Sundays is not occasional or optional, even when it would be much more convenient or comfortable to stay at home. Adela Barone, *previous page*, supports the head of her infirm mother, Maria, during worship services in Puebla, Mexico. In a meetinghouse in Detroit, Alexandria Kiel and her mother Deborah, *above*, rehearse for their ward's upcoming children's sacrament meeting. Earlier in the day, Versie Wilson shares her spiritual feelings while seated in a pew because it is difficult for her to stand or to walk. Because this meetinghouse was once a Greek Orthodox church, the pews are decorated with crosses, a common Christian symbol that is never seen in structures built for Mormon worship. As one Church authority explained: "We are grateful beyond words for the sacrifice of Jesus Christ on the cross at Calvary. But we worship a Savior who conquered death, and so we focus our attention on the eternal consequences of His life rather than on the instrument of His death."

Photographs: previous page, Robin Bowman; left and above,
Taro Yamasaki

129

Church members with disabilities provide opportunities for Latter-day Saints to serve each other. *Right,* Remo Cantergiani, who is both deaf and blind, participates in a Church meeting with the help of the interpretive signing provided by Joyanne Burdett (right) and Deborah Jamison (left). The three belong to an LDS ward in Fremont, California, that was created specifically for members with special needs.

Photograph: Kim Komenich

Church attendance offers an opportunity for friends of all ages to visit. In a meetinghouse in Salt Lake City, *below*—complete with a mural depicting Joseph Smith and the angel Moroni—Lemonte Peterson (left) and Dr. M. Lynn Bennion (right) do some catching up. And in Detroit, Michigan, *right*, Courtney Wilson and Amy Anderson share a smile and a story.

Photographs: below, Joel Sartore; right, Taro Yamasaki

Primary is the Church's organization for children, with Sunday gospel classes and weekday activities for youngsters 18 months old to 12 years of age. And throughout the world, Primary teachers use creative methods to teach their students important gospel principles. In Detroit, *above,* children learn about prophets through a song that devotes verses to Moses, Adam, and Daniel. The song urges them to "Follow the prophet . . . He knows the way." In Kenya, *right,* Anna Robert Nzibo leads her charges in rhythmic movements as they practice a new song.

Photographs: above, Taro Yamasaki; right, Lori Grinker

Local LDS congregations, called wards, are led by lay ministers who hold the title of bishop. (In the case of some smaller congregations, called branches, leaders are known as branch presidents.) They serve for several years, ministering to the spiritual and temporal needs of the members of their congregations while they continue to work in their own vocations to provide income for their families. They supervise worship services and ward activities, oversee welfare projects and disbursements, and counsel individual members in distress. After a few years, they are released to serve in other capacities in the Church, and new leaders are called to service in their place. *Above*, acting president Igor Yakushin of the Eastern Moscow Branch in Russia is seen at home enjoying a snack with his wife, Lyena, and four-year-old daughter, Agnessa. *Near right*, Yakushin, a magician by profession, entertains schoolchildren with a little magical sleight of hand. *Far right*, Bishop Virgil L. Merrill of Salt Lake City checks in on ward member Herbert Millfred.

Photographs: above and near right, Nikolai Ignatiev; far right, Joel Sartore

In the LDS meetinghouse at Tai Po, New Territories, Hong Kong, *left*, Elder John K. Carmack (left), a General Authority assigned to supervise the Church in Asia, visits with his counselor in the area presidency, Kwok Yuen Tai. General Authorities are priesthood leaders who have been called to full-time Church service. Included among these leaders are the First and Second Quorums of the Seventy. As a member of the Seventy, Elder Carmack travels throughout Asia overseeing the administration of Church programs. He is currently supervising the construction of a new LDS temple in Kowloon, which he insists will be "the most important temple built since the Salt Lake Temple because of its location in China." Elder Carmack holds a planning meeting for the new temple's open house in the offices of local Church leader Tony Wong, *above right* and *center right*. He later takes a break from his ecclesiastical duties to jog, *below right,* in the hills behind the Hong Kong apartment building where he lives.

Photographs: Doug Menuez

While worship services in local LDS meetinghouses are open to all people regardless of faithfulness or religious preference, temple worship is reserved for worthy adult members of the Church. Latter-day Saints like to say that what goes on within the walls of the temple is not secret, but it is sacred. And they are encouraged to have photographs of temples in their homes, *far right,* to remind their families of the important religious ceremonies, like marriages and baptisms, that take place within the temple walls. Non-Mormons and less-active Mormons can tour new temples during periods of public open house—as long as they don't mind wearing white booties to protect the temple carpets, *near right.* But after a temple has been officially dedicated, only those who are specifically authorized by the leaders of their local ward and stake (a group of wards) can enter. Following the open house for the Church's temple in Bountiful, Utah, workers use tiny brushes to clean and prepare the building, *below,* for its formal dedication.

Photographs: Joel Sartore

Before the San Diego Temple, *right,* was dedicated, a public open house attracted curious visitors from a variety of different religious backgrounds. *Above,* a family watches a video presentation while waiting their turn to tour. Following its dedication, the temple was closed to the public, and the significant work for which it was designed then began.

Photographs: Acey Harper

The crowning ordinance of the Church is the eternal marriage, or "sealing," of couples to each other. Because Mormons believe that such marriages will endure beyond the grave, the decision to marry is taken very seriously. From their earliest years, young Latter-day Saints are taught to prepare themselves for the blessing of temple marriage. For Jennelle and David Anderson, both 23, *left*, that preparation resulted in a joyful wedding day at the Salt Lake Temple. *Above,* two young flowergirls watch with awe—and perhaps anticipation—as another bride and groom pose for pictures outside the temple.

Photographs: left, Joel Sartore; above, Dagmar Fabricius and Randy Taylor

Perched on scaffolding 300 feet above the ground, craftsman Dave Horne applies gold leaf to a heroic-size statue of the angel Moroni, *left,* on a spire of the Church's Washington, D.C., temple, *above.* Mormons believe that Moroni was a prophet who lived on the American continent in ancient times and who, as a resurrected being, delivered to young Joseph Smith the golden plates upon which were engraved the Book of Mormon. Portrayed with a trumpet to his lips to herald the rise of Mormonism, Moroni is to some Mormons the fulfillment of St. John's prophetic vision of "another angel [flying] in the midst of heaven, having the everlasting gospel to preach unto them that dwell on the earth, and to every nation, and kindred, and tongue, and people, saying with loud voice, 'Fear God, and give glory to him; for the hour of his judgment is come; and worship him that made heaven and earth, and the sea and the fountains of waters'" (Revelations 14: 6–7).

Photographs: Mark Atkinson

147

III

Spreading the Word

The image is familiar to people all around the world: two young men in white shirts and ties, with neatly trimmed hair, pedaling their bicycles to . . . well, to wherever it is that Mormon missionaries pedal their bicycles.

Which, as it turns out, is just about everywhere.

With only a handful of exceptions, missionaries from The Church of Jesus Christ of Latter-day Saints proselytize in nearly every nation of the world. These missionaries come in all sizes, races, and socioeconomic backgrounds. They come in all ages, from teenagers to septuagenarians. They come in both genders, singly and as married couples. They voluntarily give up a year or two of their lives to go wherever their Church sends them, paying their own expenses for the privilege of being both loved and disliked, accepted and rejected, appreciated and belittled, an instrument of conversion and an object of ridicule.

Why do they do it? There are a lot of reasons—probably almost as many as there are missionaries. But there is one common thread that seems to weave its way into the fabric of every missionary's life and consciousness: a desire to serve God, the Mormon Church, and the world.

To Latter-day Saints, service in the Church and to mankind is an integral part of a theology that is based on the beliefs that "faith without works is dead" (James 3:26) and that "when ye are in the service of your fellow beings ye are only in the service of your God" (Mosiah 2:17).

That is why thousands of men and women are willing to put their personal and professional lives on hold while they share the Mormon message as missionaries. That is also why large numbers of volunteers respond almost instantly to any emergency anywhere in the world. And why Latter-day Saints care for one another through an independent welfare system that stresses self-reliance and personal responsibility. And that is why the Church and its members are involved in benevolent projects that seem to be motivated by no other reason than to make some corner of the globe a little kinder and a little sweeter.

Why do Mormons do it? Because each Church member shares the beliefs that there is a God in heaven who is kind and loving and that the family is an eternal unit, which includes the living and dead. And they also do it because they are certain that love and service are concepts that must be extended beyond the individual self to encompass all mankind.

Photograph: Acey Harper

A MINISTRY OF LOVE AND FAITH

PHOTO ESSAY
Prison Ministry

Bishop Heber Geurts, 86, arrives at the Utah State Prison in Draper early Sunday morning, *previous page,* ready to continue his 40-year ministry with the inmates. On his jacket he wears a pin that says, simply, "I care," *left,* a philosophy that has guided his volunteer service at the prison since 1955, when two men from his neighborhood were incarcerated there. "I never draw the line on race, creed, religion, or crime," Geurts says. "God didn't do it. Why should I? We're all His children." The only civilian allowed to move freely around the prison without an escort, Geurts offers casual fellowship as well as individual counseling, *right,* on his regular prison visits which he makes two and sometimes three times a week.

Photographs: Joel Sartore

Geurts, *left,* dabs at tears in his eyes as a former member of his prison "flock," Arthur Isaacson, and his wife, Cori, share an embrace during a visit in Geurts's living room in Holiday, Utah. "He never turned anyone away," Isaacson says. "He looked at the soul of every man. He was like a beam of light amongst the shadows of the inmates." The number of prisoners attending services, *below,* is irrelevant to this LDS leader. "Jesus said that a good shepherd will go out to bring in the lost sheep, even if there's only one," Geurts explains. "These men are God's lost sheep, and each one is important to Him—and to me."
Photographs: Joel Sartore

The structural organization of the Church, with its closely connected lines of stewardship and authority, makes for quick responses to emergency situations all around the world—for Mormons and non-Mormons alike. *Left,* two full-time missionaries, Elder Eric Wamsley of Laketown, Utah, and Sister Christine Wagner of Burlington, Wisconsin, help gather Barbara Burright's belongings during floods in Kingwood, Texas. *Above right,* clothing, food, and other emergency goods are packaged for shipment and stored in one of the Church's huge warehouses in Salt Lake City. From here, they can be shipped to any part of the world when a crisis arises. *Center right,* Monica Ramos sorts through items donated by Mormons from the Salt Lake area at the Church's Deseret Industries thrift store. *Below right,* shoppers select groceries at the Bishop's Storehouse, where food is available free of charge to Church members in need. Whenever possible, the recipients donate their time or skills in exchange.

Photographs: left, C. J. Walker; right, Joel Sartore

For generations, Mormon women have practiced the art of quilting, and the work they produce, *below,* is highly regarded. Quilting is a significant part of Mormon culture in that it represents an aesthetic link to the Church's pioneer past, but it is especially important as a service project. On the last Tuesday of each month, a quilting bee is held in Salt Lake City's Colonial House. Dozens of LDS women gather, *right,* to create patchwork quilts that are auctioned off, with the proceeds going to fund medical research at a local hospital.

Photographs: Dagmar Fabricius and Randy Taylor

158

The Relief Society, the world's oldest organization for women, is guided by the theme "Charity Never Faileth." And in all of its endeavors around the world, like this literacy project in Soweto, South Africa, *above*, the focus is on service. As president of the Soweto Relief Society, Julia Mavimbela helped Gloria Maguana start her own sewing business. *Below*, Mavimbela is embraced by Maguana who is soon to become a member of the local LDS congregation. In the Dominican Republic, *right*, Elder Geoff Steurer visits a Catholic nursing home as part of an ongoing project organized by the Relief Society. One of the nuns commented that other service groups come to talk with the elderly residents, "but when the Mormons come, they come to work—mopping floors, making beds, whatever needs to be done."

Photographs: above and below, Lori Grinker; right, Robin Bowman

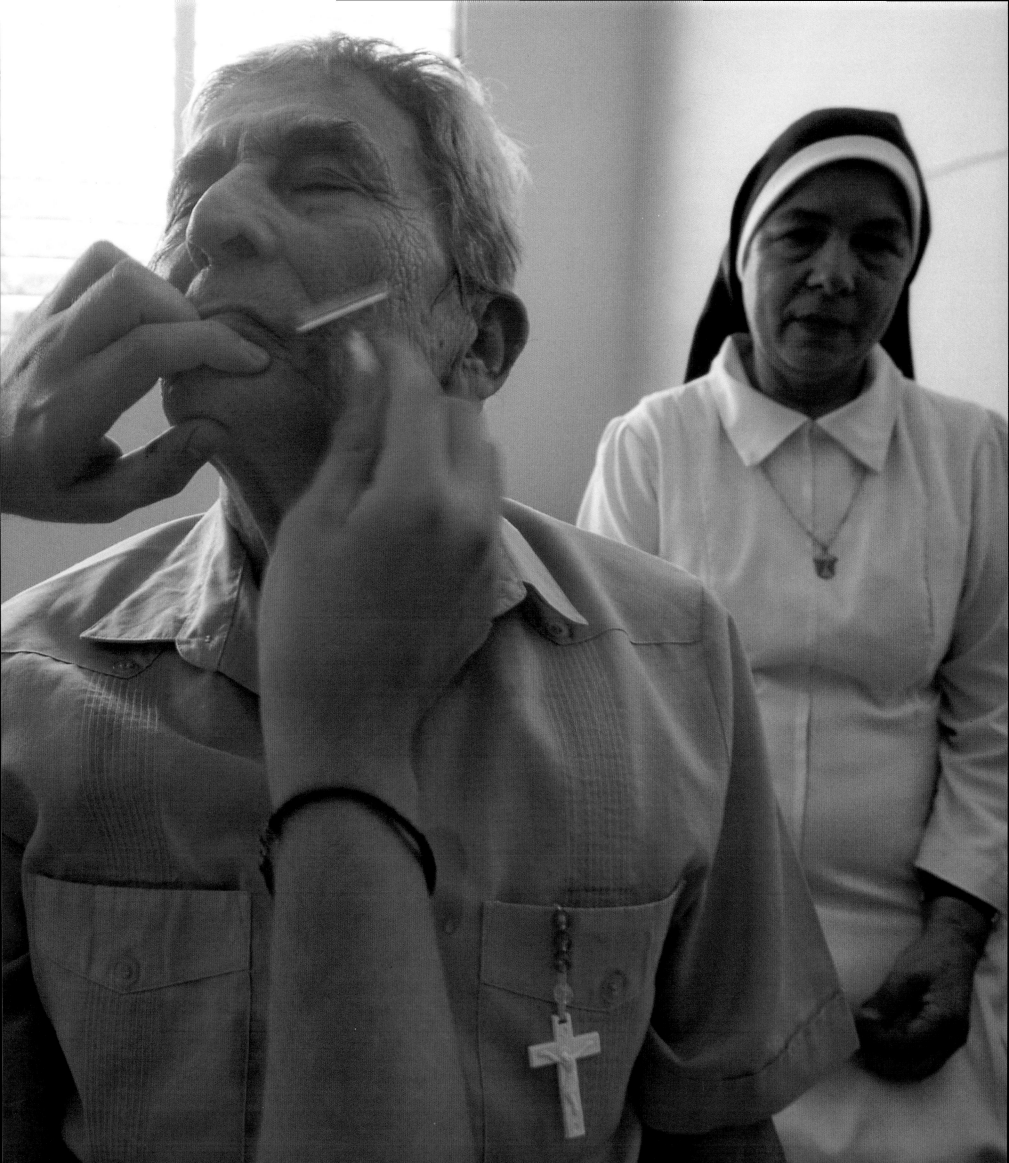

Estelle Moeck, *left,* reaches for a ripe pear at the stake welfare project in Wenatchee, Washington. Throughout the Church, congregations are involved in similar projects that are geared toward service and self-reliance. In San Diego, the project is a tuna cannery, and in Florida, it's welfare orange groves. Staffed primarily by volunteers, these projects provide much of the food that fills the Bishop's Storehouses and is made available to needy individuals around the world. On this day, some 150 volunteers gather in Wenatchee to harvest the year's crop. *Above,* after a long morning of pear picking, Randy Webb (right) joins the other volunteers for a plateful of lunch, courtesy of the local Relief Society.

Photographs: Rich Frishman

163

At six o'clock in the morning, six days a week, 91-year-old Pauolo Malupo, *left*, pedals his bike from his home in Haleiwa, Hawaii, to the place where he catches the bus that takes him to the Church's Hawaii Temple in Laie. Malupo actually uses two bicycles in his daily journey: one to shuttle him between his home and the bus stop in Haleiwa, and one to take him back and forth between the temple and the bus stop in Laie. After he spends the morning performing religious services in the temple, he changes his clothes and goes to work at a stake welfare project, *below,* near his home. *Right,* 88-year-old Elsie Hammel and a friend make flower leis on the lawn in front of the Hawaii Tabernacle in Honolulu. The leis are used as farewell greetings for young people beginning their missions, as well as for funerals.

Photographs: Robert Holmes

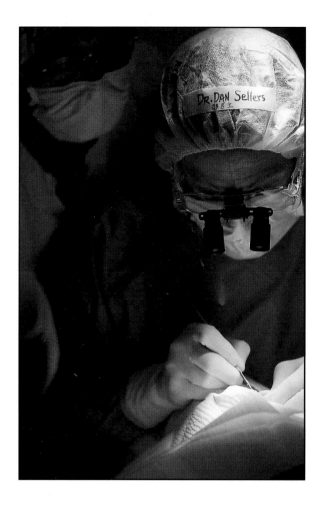

Plastic surgeon Dan Sellers of Salt Lake City is one of a number of LDS medical professionals who belong to Operation Smile, an organization that sends skilled personnel to perform life-changing reconstructive surgery on needy children in America and around the world. The physicians have treated more than 13,000 children for cleft lips and palates, burn scars, and other deformities. In Shantou, China, *left,* Dr. Sellers examines an infant with a cleft palate, while another baby, *below,* awaits his attention. *Above,* Dr. Sellers performs surgery at Shantou's University Hospital.

Photographs: Mark Atkinson

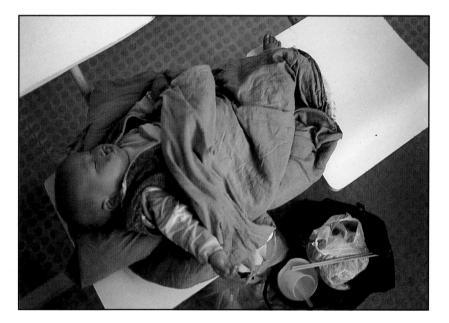

168

Convoy to Croatia

As president of the Relief Society in her ward in Sheffield, England, Carol Gray was anxious to involve her organization in benevolent service that extended beyond the members' homes and families. And so they began collecting medical supplies, baby food, and diapers for the besieged people of Bosnia and Croatia. When Gray could not find anyone to transport the donated materials, she decided to make the transcontinental journey herself, selling the family car in order to purchase one of the vans that would be needed. Gray has subsequently organized 14 trips to the small Croatian village of Rovanska, which she has personally adopted. At the Austrian border, *above left,* she is tired and frustrated as uncooperative guards delay the convoy's travel for seven hours. The group is fined for driving vehicles that are heavier than the legal limit before being sent on its way. Eventually, they arrive at Senj on the Croatian coast, where they deliver some of their goods, *below left,* and try to grab a few hours sleep in their van, *below,* after having been on the road for 24 hours straight.

Photographs: Barry Lewis

The trip to this war-ravaged area was marked by difficulty and danger, but there were experiences that fortified the travelers' faith. At one point, as the convoy was passing down a coastal road in Croatia, a trailer came loose from the van, pulling the vehicle into a 180-degree spin. Miraculously, no one was hurt and the van came out unscathed. *Above,* "Big John" Byron lifts the trailer onto one of the trucks with the help of two Croatian soldiers. After some 20 breakdowns and several close calls, the group pauses at Senj at dawn, *left,* to give thanks for their safe arrival.

Photographs: Barry Lewis

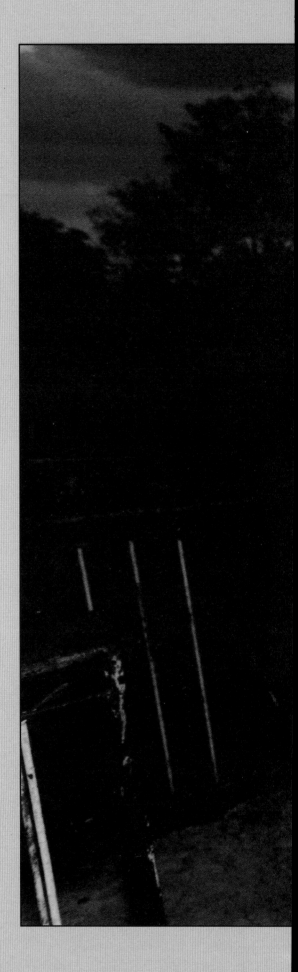

Despite the challenges of the journey, there are joyous moments when the group distributes much-needed supplies, *above* and *below.* "The end of the trip was like an emotional flood," recalls photographer Barry Lewis, who accompanied Gray on this convoy. "Tears were flowing on both sides. And even though none of us really knew what the people of Rovanska were saying, we knew what they were feeling." Gray embraces a 90-year-old woman, *right,* outside Zedar, just two miles from the front lines of military action. She recognized the woman from a previous visit and recalled that she lived alone with her cats in a burned-out house. Gray insisted the van stop so she could give the old woman food—and love.

Photographs: Barry Lewis

THE MISSION

Emissaries to Moscow

Elders Andrew Roundy, 20, and Kevin Clark, 19, gaze through a window as their train prepares to depart from Moscow's Kazansky Station, *previous page*. The missionaries are just two of several hundred young Mormons who are donating two years of their lives to help the Church establish a foothold in its most recent frontier: the countries behind what was once called the Iron Curtain. The Latter-day Saints' presence in Russia is small but growing, thanks largely to the efforts of the missionaries, who become surprisingly fluent during an eight-week language and culture course at the Missionary Training Center in Provo, Utah. *Above*, Elders Roundy and Clark prepare to share their message with Muscovites near St. Basil's Cathedral. While visiting with Church members Oleg and Dina Safronov and their two children, *above left*, the missionaries admire the medals Oleg has won for long-distance running and then share a meal, *below left*.

Photographs: Nikolai Ignatiev

For most missionaries, the two years of full-time service include a wide assortment of experiences and memories—from the deeply spiritual and profound to the lighthearted and fun. *Right,* Elder Roundy begins a day in Moscow demonstrating a decidedly American cooking technique: flipping pancakes. *Below,* the missionaries attend an LDS Christmas Eve party in Moscow and join in a game that asks members of the congregation to identify a particular elder simply by looking at his feet. *Bottom,* the day of the baptism of husband and wife Anatoli and Tamara Bardukov at a Russian bathhouse concludes with embraces and tears of joy.

Photographs: Nikolai Ignatiev

178

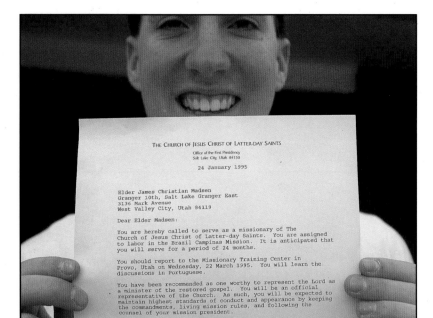

The Church of Jesus Christ of Latter-day Saints

Office of the First Presidency
Salt Lake City, Utah 84150

24 January 1995

Elder James Christian Madsen
Granger 10th, Salt Lake Granger East
3136 Mark Avenue
West Valley City, Utah 84119

Dear Elder Madsen:

You are hereby called to serve as a missionary of The
Church of Jesus Christ of Latter-day Saints. You are assigned
to labor in the Brazil Campinas Mission. It is anticipated that
you will serve for a period of 24 months.

You should report to the Missionary Training Center in
Provo, Utah on Wednesday, 22 March 1995. You will learn the
discussions in Portuguese.

You have been recommended as one worthy to represent the Lord as
a minister of the restored gospel. You will be an official
representative of the Church. As such, you will be expected to
maintain highest standards of conduct and appearance by keeping
the commandments, living mission rules, and following the
counsel of your mission president.

Two of the most eagerly anticipated events in the life of a young Latter-day Saint are the day he receives his missionary assignment from the Church's First Presidency and the day he returns home from his mission. For Jim Madsen, *left,* the mission call comes on the same day as his brother, Grant, *below right,* returns home from his mission in Brazil. The Madsen family gathers, *below,* to share these two extraordinary moments and are excited to learn that Jim is being called to the same mission Grant had just served. *Above right,* Karen Denison anxiously waits at the Salt Lake City International Airport for the return of her missionary son, Matt, from his two-year stint in Chicago.

Photographs: Joel Sartore

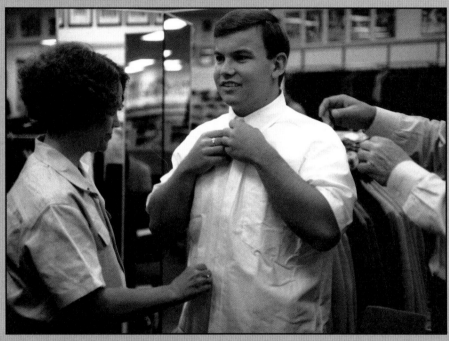

PHOTO ESSAY

The Making of a Missionary

The transition from teenager to full-time Church missionary can be a little overwhelming, both for the new missionary and for his family. But it is usually an exciting experience that is keenly anticipated. *Above left,* Brigham Wise and his family gather in their home near San Francisco to open Brigham's missionary call from the Church's First Presidency. They learn that he will be going to Thailand. Pre-mission preparations include shopping for suits, white shirts, ties, and other clothing essentials at Mr. Mac's, *center left,* a Salt Lake City clothier that specializes in outfitting missionaries. *Above right,* Brigham is "set apart" as a missionary by his father, Jeff (left), and Stake President Boyd C. Smith. From that moment on, Brigham Wise is "Elder Wise." Before embarking on his two-year mission, he says an emotional good-bye to his family, *below right.* First he will spend eight weeks at the Missionary Training Center in Provo, where he will work, worship, study, and pray, *below left,* with other new missionaries bound for Thailand.

Photographs: Acey Harper

In Thailand, Elder Wise is assigned to work with Elder J. Bradley Wagstaff in the village of Roi Et, where he puts into practice the language and cultural training he received at the Missionary Training Center. *Below,* Elder Wise shares his message with Buddhist monks in a monastery near Roi Et. *Right,* the missionaries meet with a Thai family in the space underneath their house, which is built on stilts, as is customary in the area. It has been about three months since Brigham received his missionary call, but his family and friends in northern California seem a lifetime away.

Photographs: Acey Harper

Although a mission is filled with long periods of hard work and sacrifice, one day of each week is devoted to maintenance activities like shopping, cleaning, letter writing, and sight-seeing. Commonly known as P-Day, or Preparation Day, it is a time that is appreciated. *Below,* missionaries at Manila's Missionary Training Center wash their clothes in traditional Filipino fashion. *Right,* preparation of another sort occurs each night, as missionaries in New York City kneel to pray before going to bed.

Photographs: below, Paul Chesley; right, Ed Kashi

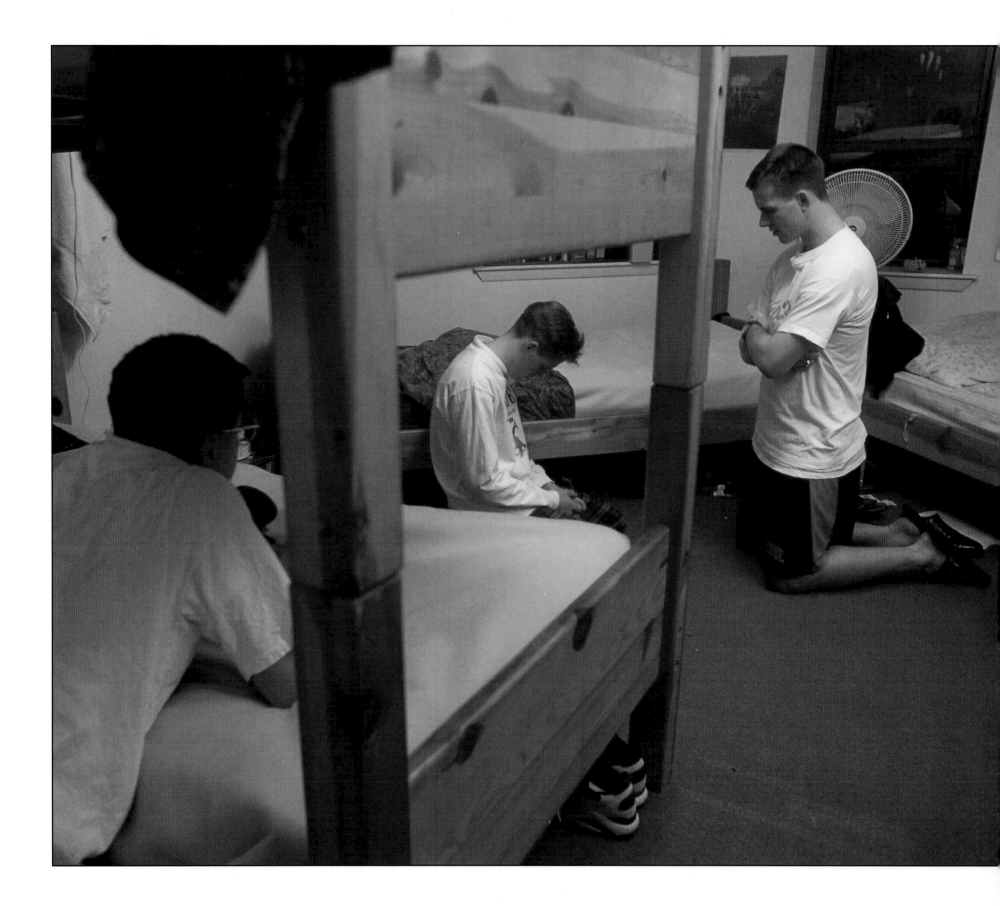

Missionaries throughout the world are required to spend at least four hours each week in nonproselytizing community service. For Elders Joshua T. Williams and Brian E. Hawkins, two missionaries in Warsaw, Poland, that means serving in this Catholic-sponsored soup kitchen in a poor Warsaw neighborhood. *Right,* Elder Hawkins receives a tray of bread from Sister Jozefa, the nun who is in charge of the project. *Below,* two missionaries in Dublin, Ireland, let their hair down—such as it is— during a service project on behalf of the residents of St. Vincents' Home, a Catholic-run center for mentally handicapped adults.

Photographs: below, Gideon Mendel; right, Tomasz Tomaszewski

Door-to-door "tracting," or cold contacting, isn't necessarily a favorite proselytizing technique among Mormon missionaries. Nor is it considered the most effective means of sharing the gospel message. Still, it is a time-honored method of reaching out to individuals and families, and most missionaries spend a considerable amount of time doing it. *Left,* Elders Steven Wright and Robert Palfreyman visit a man in Belize who has expressed an interest in the Church and invite him to attend services with them later that morning. *Below,* Sisters Shelby Leishman of Rexburg, Idaho, and Suzanne Wilson of Everett, Washington, visit a home in Hartford, Connecticut, as part of their mission service.

Photographs: left, Acey Harper; below, Nina Barnett

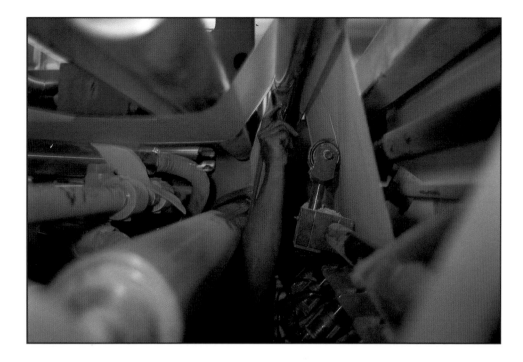

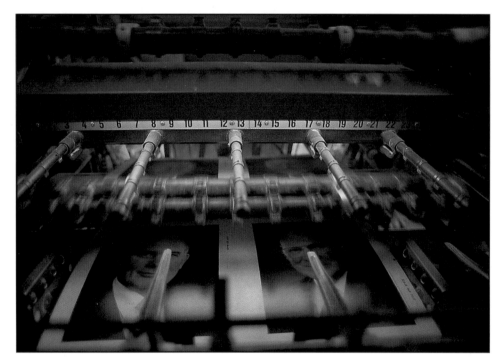

Because LDS missionaries take the gospel to all parts of the globe, religious materials must be available in as many as 90 different languages and dialects. Every year, the Salt Lake Printing Services print more than 3 million volumes of the scriptures, nearly 7 million handbooks, 14 million magazines, and 70 million posters, *top* and *above. Right,* a Church employee pedals his way through one of the acres of aisles in the Printing Services' distribution center, from which materials are shipped to LDS members throughout the world.

Photographs: Joel Sartore

When most people think of Mormon missionaries, they probably think of clean-cut young men in white shirts and ties. But more and more retired individuals and couples are leaving their homes and grandchildren to spend from six months to three years serving in locations around the world. Photographs of all the couples from the local ward who are currently working as missionaries are displayed, *above,* in a Salt Lake City meetinghouse. *Right,* Elder Rinaldo Denison plays with young Sarah Romann in the Kenyan village of Nthongoni. The children of LDS missionaries sometimes become involved in Church work before they are old enough to begin their own mission. *Below,* 13-year-old Kelli Taggart, the daughter of a mission couple in the Philippines, reads to children in Manila as part of a village literacy program.

Photographs: above, Joel Sartore; below, Paul Chesley; right, Lori Grinker

For LDS missionaries, the setting for a discussion about the Church isn't as important as the spiritual feeling that is present. *Right,* even an abandoned Chevy by the side of a dirt road in Belize can be a good place to talk if people are sincerely interested in what the missionaries have to say. *Below,* Elders Wright and Palfreyman share the Church's message with recent convert Jose Orlando Escobar in his home in Succotz, Belize.

Photographs: Acey Harper

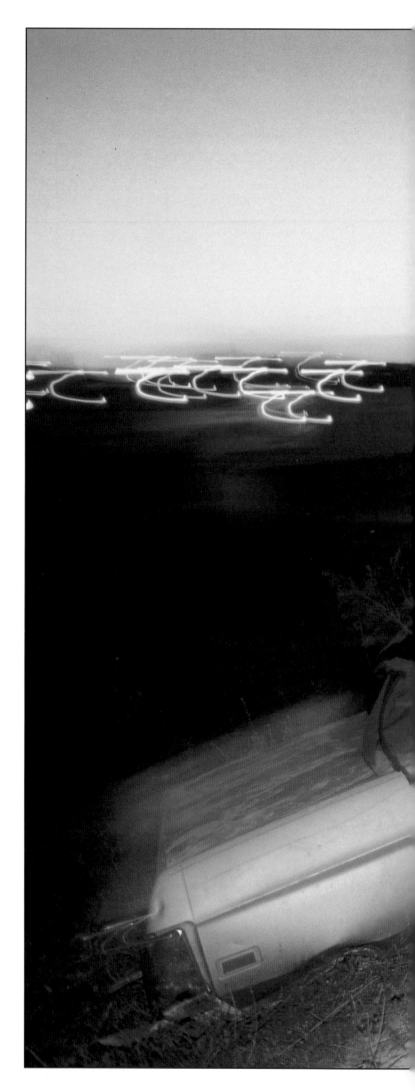

Elders John Hansen and Val Nelson, *right,* pause to bless the evening meal of rabbit stew at the home of LDS member and community matriarch Sheila Reid in Gulargambone, New South Wales, Australia. After dinner, *above,* Reid's grandchildren huddle around the glowing warmth of a campfire. Both members and "investigators" (individuals who are interested in learning about the Church but who have not yet joined) often invite missionaries assigned to their area into their homes, to share meals and family life.

Photographs: Emmanuel Santos

Looking from Kowloon across the harbor to a mist-shrouded Hong Kong, Elders David Ferronato and Jonathan Garriot, *right,* prepare to board a train that will take them into the New Territories, where they will work for the day. Some of the people they call on when they arrive are willing to talk to them, such as this woman, *below,* but most are not, *bottom.* "It's tough to find people who are interested in what we have to say," Elder Garriot remarks. "But we keep trying."

Photographs: Doug Menuez

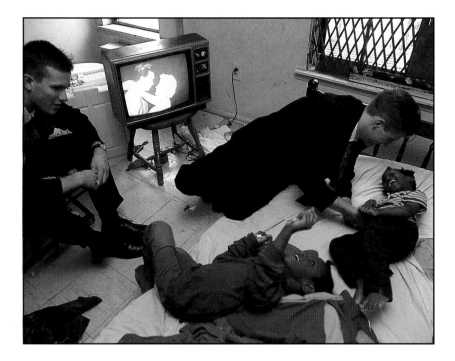

Walking past graffiti-covered walls in the Bronx, *right,* Elders Ryan Werlich of Diamond Springs, California, and Paul Schwitzer of Salt Lake City tract in New York. Later in the day, they enjoy a family home evening, *above,* with members Sharon Wilson and her children, Demildra, two, Stephanie, four, and Mustafa, ten. *Below,* Ruby Kemp, who is deaf, gets a helping hand from Elder Brandon Arthur as she prepares to go out shopping. Some missionaries who work with the hearing impaired learn American Sign Language in an intensive course at a Missionary Training Center. Others, like Elder Arthur, whose father is deaf, and his partner, Elder Maldanado (not shown), grew up using sign language, which they can now use to reach out to a population that is often marginalized.

Photographs: Ed Kashi

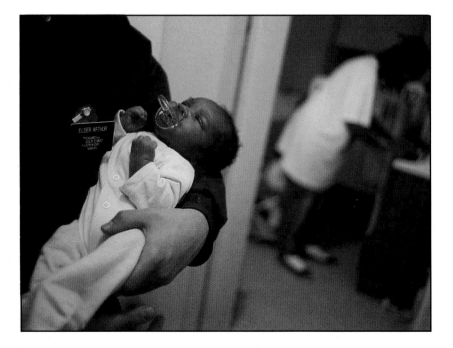

On a mission in the Dominican Republic, Sister Amy Lyn Kondris of Grain Valley, Missouri, stops at the home of Dolores Santana, *right,* to ask directions. Sister Kondris and her companion, Sister Hae Ryong Lee of Renton, Washington, were pleasantly surprised when Dolores asked them to stop and share the LDS message with her and her family. Eventually, the family accepted the missionaries' invitation to read the Book of Mormon and to attend church services the following week. *Above,* beneath the protective covering of mosquito netting, Sisters Kondris and Lee study the scriptures for up to an hour every morning. *Below,* the young women play with Alfredo Castillo, four, and his two-year-old brother, Carlos Javier.

Photographs: Robin Bowman

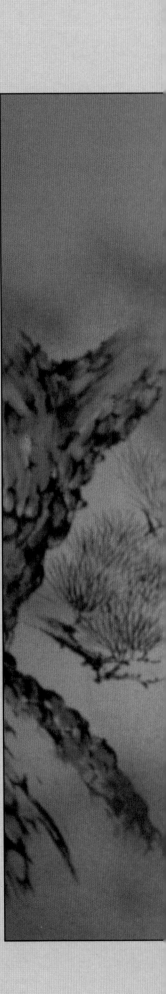

In addition to sharing their message with all who will listen, missionaries are also taught to appreciate the culture and the people of the countries where they are called to serve. Elders Brandon Pack and Tyler Slade, both from Salt Lake City, enjoy a meal, *right,* in Yonezawa, Japan, with Yukiko Nihei (center), to whom they are teaching English, her brother, Takeshi (second from left), and his wife, Yoko (left). Later that evening, *above,* the missionaries dance during the Bon Odori festivities, celebrating the traditional Buddhist Feast of the Dead. This festival, which honors deceased ancestors, echoes the Church's teachings about the eternal family unit and the kindred dead. *Left,* Elder Slade shares a cherished possession: a Japanese–English dictionary that was given to him by his grandfather, who worked with expatriate Japanese during his mission in Hawaii before World War II.

Photographs: Torin Boyd

In Kenya, Elder Albert Kemp of Kansas City, Missouri, is partnered with Elder Prince Henry Omondi, who was born in this East African country. Omondi is one of the hundreds of missionaries who are called to serve in their homelands, bringing language skills and cultural understanding to their work with American missionaries. In their simple kitchen, *top left,* Kemp and Omondi prepare a meal of vegetables and *ugali,* a regional staple food of cornmeal mixed in boiling water. *Bottom left,* the two men ride their bicycles 45 minutes deep into the bush country of Kenya to the village of Mbukoni. There they teach the family of Julius Mutua, *center left.* Mutua's son Joseph has been a Mormon for eight years. The culmination of the missionaries' work is the baptism of a young man, *right,* which takes place in a cement font under the watchful eye of his father and curious neighborhood children.

Photographs: Lori Grinker

There is nothing more rewarding for missionaries than to watch someone they have taught and served and loved accept their message and enter into the waters of baptism. In some missions, such baptisms are commonplace, while in others they are quite rare. *Right,* Elder Brigham Wise baptizes an eight-year-old girl in Roi Et, in northeastern Thailand. In the azure waters of the Caribbean, Matilde Batista de Pimentel, *following page,* exults in her baptism at Playa Acapulco in Sabana de La Mar, in the Dominican Republic, while Sister Hae Ryong Lee (left) looks on.

Photographs: right, Acey Harper; following page, Robin Bowman

Images of Faith

by ROGER ROSENBLATT

The first images of the Mormon faith that I saw were verbal. A man named Jon Beck Shank, a poet and a member of The Church of Jesus Christ of Latter-day Saints, came to teach English at my New York City high school when I was in my senior year. None of us had ever seen a teacher as brilliant and inventive as Shank. He taught us the power and the meaning of words, and he was the first bona fide poet most of us had ever met.

Much of Shank's poetry was grounded in his Mormon upbringing, and several of his poems addressed the experience directly. "Did I not declare my word unto you . . . even as one speaking out of the dust?" is a quotation from the Book of Mormon that serves as the title of one of his poems. The fourth stanza reads as follows:

> People themselves glow in the glass air,
>> slowly
> Donning the lucent word as an incandescent
>> sheath
> Their waking dreams are become self-resolutions
>> of strength.

That image, of people glowing in the glass air and wearing the fragile armor of the word of God, was the first way I saw the Latter-day Saints.

Like Joseph Smith, who wrote of "the evidence of things not seen," Jon Beck Shank believed that the temporal world was infused with, indeed illuminated by, the spiritual, and that the life one can actually see is only made valuable by the life one dreams. "All things to me are spiritual, and not at any time have I given unto you a law which is temporal." This was offered to Smith in a revelation in September 1830. And what it seems to mean is that every earthly activity is endowed with spiritual significance. Faith finds its form in everything—which suggests that every act, no matter how casual or commonplace, is an image or demonstration of faith. (Oddly, this means that those who are not believers can also be images of faith, at least when they are beheld by those who are.) The eye of the beholder who believes, observes, and detects the spiritual in all temporal activities thus endows everything with faith. Like a celestial camera, it sees that which is there and that which is not.

The symbology of religions takes its various shapes in crescents, stars, and crosses. But more complicated and mysterious is the idea that the faithful are living symbols themselves; that the human icons, however stumbling and confused, are the true signs of any faith; and that their "self-resolutions of strength," as Shank put it, constitute continuous reform and affirmation. By their belief, and by the actions and rituals that fortify their belief, they become the temple, the robe, the history, and the future.

This idea may intensify the pictorial images that appear in this book. For example, there are several photographs in the preceding pages of people in the act of praying. A boy kneels beside his bed, rests his head on his folded arms, and closes his eyes. Members of a Dominican family of five sit upright in bed and close their eyes. An Irish boxer and his son press together, eyes closed. A group of students from the Brigham Young University Jerusalem Center bow their heads in a bus near Cairo, Egypt, their eyes also closed. A prisoner lowers his head in a chapel pew. We see only his upper back and the number on his shirt. We must assume that his eyes, too, are closed in prayer.

Why do they do that—close their eyes in prayer? To hunker down? To shut out the external world? That is fairly easily done. But what do they see? In the nothing before them, in the multicolored darkness created by the veil of the inside of their eyelids, what do they see? Their souls? Perhaps, but rarely. God Himself? Perhaps, but more rarely still.

What they see, most likely, is themselves in prayer, as if in the act of communicating with God they have stepped out of their bodies and observed their lives. In prayer, each becomes an image of faith in the middle of an act of faith.

Smith taught that every person is an incubative god and that God, too, had achieved divinity by progressing through stages of endurance and knowledge. Exaltation, Smith believed, awaited those who followed a similar path. Thus the Mormon doctrine of "eternal progression." According to this doctrine, human potential is without limits. To pray to God is to express divine aspiration, which requires a rapt concentration on one's conduct, ambitions, emotions—on one's entire being. Who would not close his eyes?

Now consider the pictures of the various baptisms—the immersion of children and adult converts in the cold water of their spiritual awakenings. Like the pictures of the people praying, these, too, seem simple enough. But baptism among Latter-day Saints has a double resonance. If everyone were capable of eternal progression, what allowance could be made for those who died before they had received the restored gospel—including ancestors who went back centuries? This question, posed in the earliest days of the founding of the Church, led to yet another doctrine special to it—that of the salvation of the dead.

In a funeral sermon in August 1840, Smith first spoke publicly of a "baptism for the dead." Initially, this was performed in the upper valley of the Mississippi River at the settlement in Nauvoo, Illinois, with living Church members serving as proxies. Soon afterward, the ordinance was moved to a font inside the temple, where it remains today.

Essentially, baptism was and is an expression of exaltation—a concept so inclusive that it transcends the boundaries of mortality. Except for a fleeting New Testament reference in First Corinthians (15:29), the idea of baptism after death seems to have been first stated as a religious idea by Joseph Smith. And by this ordinance, he extended the baptism of the child to a baptism of all life. In the photograph of the boy in Alaska bending backward in the water holding his nose—that is, stopping his breath—one sees the baptism of birth and death together.

Prayer, baptism, funerals, weddings; the laying-on of hands; the choir singing; a congregation in the act of "sustaining"—all are seen and bear the evidence of things not seen.

Among all these strong images, one of the most memorable appears so ordinary, it could be a family snapshot: at General Conference, three Church members stand together in the Salt Lake Tabernacle, responding to something funny. The man on the left is smiling; the man on the right is helpless with laughter; the man in the center has the mischievous, satisfied look of someone who knows that he has just said something hilarious. I cannot fully say why this photograph leaps out at me as an image of faith. I think it may be the graceful easiness of it, the fellowship of the men in one another's company as they stand in this historic building. These Latter-day Saints are not owned by the Tabernacle, they own it. Their faith and the faith of their ancestors built it. It is a place where they can be themselves, which is to say, their best selves.

Their faces take me back to Shank's lines: "People themselves glow in the glass air, slowly / Donning the lucent word as an incandescent sheath." Clearly, the moment of delight is not a formal holy moment; but the naturalness of the laughter, the friendship it signifies, is sacred and creates its own light. ("All things to me are spiritual.") This is what it must mean to live well in the presence of God—people reveling in the surprise of being alive.

In this book, there are photographs of children playing on a trampoline in Nevada's Big Smoky Valley, a loving couple swinging together in adjacent hammocks in Brazil, and an alert-eyed Peruvian boy shining his shoes. All ordinary acts, plain as sunlight. They are images that affirm faith in The Church of Jesus Christ of Latter-day Saints and in life itself. One might even say that they affirm God's faith in the world He made. In any case, what matters most in these images are the things unseen; and what is most real is the life that is guessed at.

Shank used to have us do an exercise in his English class to show us the difference between using the nearly right word and using the exactly right word. He would give us a passage of poetry with an essential word omitted and ask us to figure out—by assessing the context, tone, and rhythm of the rest of the passage—what was missing. The point of the exercise was not to hit the word on the nose (though it was fun whenever that happened) but to get as close as possible.

The strange beauty of the exercise came from looking at the blank space where the exactly right word had been and where our newly arrived at words were yet to be. In that nothingness was everything possible. What was absent was palpably present. And while Shank never said so, I always wondered if he thought that the blank space was not, in fact, better than the word that had been there and the word that would be. I wondered if he thought that the emptiness was closer to the mark than anything that could fill it—because the space represented the evidence of the thing not seen. Yet it was there.

PHOTOGRAPHERS

MARK ATKINSON
Atkinson is a commercial and editorial photographer based in Norfolk, Virginia, and Washington, D.C. His work has appeared in *Time, Newsweek, Washingtonian, Esquire, The New York Times Magazine,* and *The Washington Post.* His photograph appears on the cover of *The Mission: Inside the Church of Jesus Christ of Latter-day Saints.*

NINA BARNETT
A freelance photographer based in New York City, Barnett specializes in location assignments for magazines and corporations. Her work, which includes environmental, lifestyle, industrial, and architectural photography, has appeared in such publications as *Fortune, Newsweek,* and *Money.*

ROBIN BOWMAN ▲
Bowman is a New York–based photojournalist who freelances for most major magazines. Recent assignments have taken her from Bosnia to Guatemala for *People,* from Finland to Jamaica for *Travel Holiday,* and to Nepal for *Life.* Last year, she spent time with the Zapatistas in the jungles of Chiapas, Mexico, made trips to Haiti, and completed a book on dogs and their owners.

TORIN BOYD
A veteran of many *Day in the Life* books, Boyd began his career at the age of 17 as a surfing photographer in Florida. Now based in Tokyo, he contributes to *Fortune, Newsweek, Time, U.S. News & World Report,* and several Japanese magazines.

PAUL CHESLEY ▲
A freelancer with the National Geographic Society since 1975, Chesley is also a frequent contributor to *Fortune, Geo, Travel & Leisure, Life,* and *Stern.* Museums in London, Tokyo, and New York have held solo exhibitions of his work.

KEITH DANNEMILLER
Dannemiller is a freelance photojournalist based in Mexico City. He currently represents Saba Press Photos in Mexico and Latin America. His work has been exhibited in various galleries and has appeared in the *San Francisco Chronicle, Time, Newsweek, The New York Times, Business Week, Forbes,* and *Texas Monthly.*

THOMAS EPTING
A New York–based freelance photographer, Epting is a recent graduate of Brigham Young University's photography department. While at BYU, his editorial and sports photography was widely published in campus and regional publications.

DAGMAR FABRICIUS AND RANDY TAYLOR
After working for years as individual freelance photographers on contract for Photoreporters, Visions, Associated Press, Sygma, and Black Star, Fabricius and Taylor formally became a team in 1987, when they cofounded International Color Stock, Inc. Specializing in people on location, Fabricius and Taylor have had their photographs published by most major publications in the United States and abroad.

RICH FRISHMAN
Frishman has been a newspaper photojournalist since 1973. His work appears regularly in *Life, Time, Newsweek, U.S. News & World Report, Money, Business Week,* and *Forbes.*

LORI GRINKER
Grinker's work has taken her to the Middle East, Southeast Asia, Eastern Europe, Africa, and throughout the United States. Her photos have been exhibited in museums in Paris, Amsterdam, and New York and have been featured in *Life, The New York Times Magazine, Newsweek, People, Stern,* and *Geo.*

ACEY HARPER ▲
Harper is a freelance photographer and picture editor based in Tiburon, California. He has traveled worldwide for such clients as *People, National Geographic,* and *USA Today,* and his work was recently selected for the cover of *A Day in the Life of Israel.* He is currently managing director of Reportáge Stock and served as director of photography for *The Mission: Inside The Church of Jesus Christ of Latter-day Saints.*

ROBERT HOLMES ▼
Holmes won the Society of American Travel Writers' Travel Photographer of the Year award in 1990 and 1992. His work regularly appears in major travel publications, including *National Geographic, Geo, Travel & Leisure,* and *Islands.* He has 15 books in print, and his photos have been exhibited widely in both corporate and museum collections.

NIKOLAI IGNATIEV
Born in Moscow in 1955 and drafted into the Soviet army in 1977, Ignatiev served in Afghanistan for two years as a Farsi interpreter. In 1987, he joined the British agency Network Photographers. He has worked on assignment for *Time, Life, The New York Times, Stern,* and *Geo.*

ED KASHI ▲
Kashi is a freelance photojournalist based in San Francisco. His work has appeared in *National Geographic* (including two cover stories), *Time, Fortune, Geo, Life, Newsweek, Forbes, Vanity Fair,* and *The New York Times Magazine.* His most recent book, *When the Borders Bleed: The Struggle of the Kurds* was published by Pantheon Books in 1994.

TIM KELLY
Kelly has worked for *The Salt Lake Tribune* for the past 27 years and is affiliated with Black Star photo agency. His photographs have appeared in *Time, Newsweek, The New York Times, Fortune, Forbes, Business Week, Der Spiegel, Boys' Life,* and a variety of computer magazines.

KIM KOMENICH
Since 1982, Komenich has been a staff photographer for the *San Francisco Examiner,* and in 1987 he received the Pulitzer Prize for his coverage of the revolution in the Philippines. His freelance work appears in such magazines as *Time, Newsweek,* and *U.S. News & World Report.*

OLIVIER LAUDE
Born in France, Laude is a freelance photographer currently living in San Francisco. He has worked extensively throughout Asia, Europe, and North and Central America, covering stories on undocumented immigrants, youth gangs, and rural life in China. His work has appeared in *Time, Business Week,* and *U.S. News & World Report.*

VERA LENTZ
Lentz was born in Peru and has lived in Europe and the United States. She freelances for major U.S. and international publications. At present she is completing a book on Peru for W. W. Norton. She is associated with Black Star photo agency in New York.

ANDY LEVIN
Levin is a New York–based freelance photographer who contributes frequently to *Life* and *People.* He received top honors in the National Press Photographers Association Pictures of the Year competition in 1985 for his essay on a Nebraska farm family and won similar honors in 1986.

BARRY LEWIS
Lewis was a founding member of the Network Photographers agency. He works for *Life, Geo,* the London *Sunday Times,* and *The Observer* and has photos on display in several American and British museums. He was the recipient of the World Press Photo Foundation's Oskar Barnack award.

TONY MCDONOUGH
Based in Australia, McDonough was a photojournalist for *The Sunday Independent* and the London *Sunday Times* before pursuing a freelance career. Through his agencies, Sydney Freelance, Camera Press, Sport: the Library, and Allsport, McDonough has covered assignments for Australia's *Who Weekly, Time, The Bulletin,* and various other newspapers and magazines.

FOREST MCMULLIN
McMullin has been a freelance commercial and editorial photographer since 1980 and is now a contract photographer with Black Star. His work has appeared in *Time, Audubon, USA Today, Forbes, Scientific American, Esquire,* and *People.*

GIDEON MENDEL
Since 1987, Mendel has been a freelance photographer working for such publications as *Stern, Time, Newsweek, Rolling Stone, U.S. News & World Report,* and *L'Express.* In 1992, he won a World Press Photo award for his story on the immigration of Ethiopian and Soviet Jews to Israel during the Gulf War. He is currently a member of the London-based agency Network Photographers.

DOUG MENUEZ ▲
Since 1982, Menuez has worked on assignment worldwide for *Time, Life, Newsweek, U.S. News & World Report, Fortune, USA Today,* and other publications, covering news, features, and sports. In 1987, he founded Reportáge, an agency specializing in black-and-white photo essays for corporations. Menuez coproduced *Fifteen Seconds: The Great California Earthquake of 1989* and in 1993 published *Defying Gravity: The Making of Newton.*

CLAUS MEYER
The winner of many prizes and awards, Meyer was selected in 1985 by *Communications World* as one of the top annual-report photographers in the world. His excellence in color photography has been recognized by Kodak and Nikon, and in 1981 he won a Nikon International Grand Prize. In 1993, he published a book on the Amazon, and has several books on Brazil to his credit.

MATTHEW NAYTHONS ▲
Prior to forming Epicenter Communications, Dr. Matthew Naythons led parallel lives—working shifts in hospital emergency rooms and traveling around the world as an award-winning photojournalist for *Time* magazine. He covered the fall of Saigon, the Jonestown massacre, and the Nicaraguan revolution, among other stories.

JONATHAN OLLEY
Olley is a freelance photographer and a member of the London-based Network Photographers agency. He has won several awards for his work, including a Nikon Press Award, and *The Observer*'s David Hodge Memorial Award for his work in war-torn Sarajevo. His photos have been published in such publications as the *Boston Globe, Paris Match, L'Express, Time,* and *Fortune.*

DREW PERINE
Currently a staff photographer for *The Herald* in Everett, Washington, Perine graduated from the University of Missouri School of Journalism and has worked as a staff photographer and director of photography for several newspapers. His work has appeared in *Newsweek, National Wildlife,* and *Ebony.*

MARK PHILBRICK
Philbrick is University Photographer for Brigham Young University. His photos have appeared in *National Geographic, The New York Times Magazine, USA Today,* and *Newsweek.*

KERI PICKETT ▲
Currently based in Minneapolis, where she was raised, Pickett has received photography awards from the Bush Foundation, the Minnesota State Arts Board, the Jerome Foundation, and the National Endowment for the Arts. Her photos have been published in *The New York Times Magazine, Newsweek, Life, Stern,* and *People.*

ALON REININGER
One of the original members of Contact Press Images, Reininger won the Press Photo of the Year award from the World Press Photo Foundation in 1986 and the Philippe Halsman Award for photojournalism in 1987. He is a regular contributor to *Time, Life, Fortune,* and the London *Sunday Times.*

RICK RICKMAN
During the five years he worked for *The Des Moines Register*, Rickman was named Iowa Photographer of the Year three times. In 1985, he won a Pulitzer Prize for coverage of the 1984 Summer Olympics and was chosen California Photographer of the Year.

BARBARA RIES ▲
Ries is a freelance photographer based in Washington, D.C. A graduate of the University of Missouri School of Journalism, her assignments have taken her to China, Central America, and the former Soviet Union. Her work has appeared in *Time, Fortune, Business Week,* the *Los Angeles Times,* and *USA Today.*

EMMANUEL SANTOS
A native of the Philippines, Santos now resides in Melbourne, Australia, where he works as a freelance photographer for *Time* (Australia), *BART,* the *Impressions* magazines of Tokyo, and the Gamma Press Paris agency. His photographs have been shown in nearly a dozen solo exhibitions throughout Asia.

JOEL SARTORE
Born and raised in Nebraska, Sartore worked for the *Wichita Eagle* for six years as a photographer and then as director of photography. Since 1991, he has been a contract photographer for *National Geographic.*

PHIL SCHERMEISTER
As a freelance photographer for *National Geographic,* Schermeister has traveled across North America working on projects such as the Tarahumara Indians of Mexico and the Pony Express. His photographs have appeared in a wide variety of publications, including *Time, Life, Geo,* and the *San Francisco Examiner.*

JAN SONNENMAIR
Sonnenmair is a freelance photojournalist living in Los Angeles. Her work appears regularly in *Life, Time, Newsweek, People, Business Week,* and *Modern Maturity.* She is currently working on a photo documentary on children with AIDS, for which she previously won the 1993 Budapest Award at the World Press Photo Foundation competition.

WOLFGANG STECHE
Based in Hamburg, Germany, Steche is a member of Visum Agency. His major focuses are on environmental contamination and conservation technology, and he has freelanced for several magazines, including *Geo, Stern, Fortune, Time,* and *Der Spiegel.*

TOMASZ TOMASZEWSKI
Tomaszewski has contributed to more than a dozen books and to such publications as *National Geographic, Fortune, Vogue, Elle,* the London *Sunday Times, The New York Times, U.S. News & World Report,* and *Geo.* He is currently based in Warsaw, Poland.

C. J. WALKER ▲
Currently a freelance photojournalist based in southern Florida, Walker divides his time between editorial assignments and architectural photography. He has worked for *The Miami Herald, Palm Beach Post, Palm Beach Life, Florida Trend,* and *People,* as well as other national magazines.

TARO YAMASAKI
A freelance photographer since 1983, Yamasaki received the 1982 Pulitzer Prize for a week-long series about life inside the world's largest walled prison. Currently a contributing photographer at *People,* he also works on assignment for *Life, Time,* and *Forbes.*

WRITERS AND CONTRIBUTORS

Writers

GORDON B. HINCKLEY, *introduction*
President Gordon B. Hinckley is the world leader of The Church of Jesus Christ of Latter-day Saints. Prior to his ordination to that position in March 1995, he served 14 years as a counselor in the First Presidency, the top governing body of the Church, and for 20 years prior to that as a member of the Quorum of the Twelve Apostles. He has received numerous academic honors, including the Distinguished Alumni Award from the University of Utah and five honorary doctorates. Other honors include the Silver Buffalo Award of the Boy Scouts of America, and a distinguished citizen award from the National Conference of Christians and Jews for his contributions to tolerance and understanding in the world.

ROGER ROSENBLATT, *epilogue*
Rosenblatt is a contributing editor to *The New York Times Magazine, Vanity Fair, The New Republic,* and *Men's Journal,* as well as a regular essayist on *The MacNeil/Lehrer News Hour* on PBS. His journalistic career includes positions as literary editor for *The New Republic,* columnist for *The Washington Post,* essayist and senior writer for *Time* magazine, and columnist and editor-at-large for *Life* magazine. A Fulbright Scholar, he holds a Ph.D. in English and American Literature from Harvard University. He has written five books, including *Children of War,* which was published in seven languages and won the Robert F. Kennedy Book Prize in 1984.

JOSEPH WALKER, *introductory essays and captions*
Walker writes a nationally syndicated newspaper column called "ValueSpeak" and is the editor of *Pioneer,* a magazine for the National Society of the Sons of Utah Pioneers. A native of Utah, he attended both the University of Utah and Brigham Young University, where he won national honors for student journalism. He was a reporter for Salt Lake City's *Deseret News* for 10 years, and is now in charge of media efforts and employee communications at Utah's Geneva Steel Corporation. As a life-long Latter-day Saint, he has served as a full-time missionary in southern California and as a bishop and counselor in a stake presidency.

Editor

KATHERINE BALL ROSS
Ross began her publishing career at Time-Life Books, working on the final volume of the Life *World Library.* With the exception of a few years in London, working at Marshall Cavenish and I.P.C., she has lived in New York City, where she has held senior editorial positions on a number of magazines published by Hearst and Conde-Nast. In addition to being a contributing editor to two national magazines, she is a freelance book editor on topics that include philosophy, psychoanalysis, and medical politics.

Art Director

ALEX CASTRO
Castro's career includes book and exhibition design as well as innovative work in sculpture and architecture. In 1977, he founded CASTRO/ARTS, a firm specializing in design for the arts. He has designed more than 100 photography and art books and museum exhibitions, including the exhibitions and accompanying books for the Corcoran Gallery's *The Indelible Image: War Photography,* for National Geographic's *Odyssey,* and for *Lee Miller: Photographer.* In addition to nearly a dozen exhibitions of his own work, his sculpture and drawings are in the permanent collections of several museums. In 1992, he designed the American Visionary Art Museum in Baltimore and is presently at work on the design of the National Museum in Kuwait.

Picture Editors

SANDRA EISERT
Eisert has been a picture editor on over 40 books. She has worked for four major metropolitan newspapers, two magazines, a wire service, and the White House. Eisert has judged all three major international photojournalism competitions and has won scores of national and international awards for her design and picture editing work.

KATHLEEN HENNESSY
Hennessy is currently the picture editor at the White House, working with the four staff photographers who document the President and First Lady. Previously, she was the picture editor for the *Washingtonian,* and for *USA Today.* She earned a BFA in photography from Arizona State University.

LARRY NIGHSWANDER
Nighswander has served as assistant director of the illustrations department of *National Geographic,* as the picture editor of *The Columbus Dispatch,* and as director of photography at *The Washington Times* and *The Cleveland Press.* In 1993, he received the Magazine Picture Editor of the Year award from the University of Missouri/National Press Photographers Association.

GEORGE WEDDING
A freelance photojournalist, writer, and publishing consultant, Wedding has served as director of photography at *The Sacramento Bee* and as a picture editor on several photographic books, including *Fifteen Seconds: The Great California Earthquake of 1989.* He has also worked as a photographer at the *San Jose Mercury News.* In 1980, he was named Newspaper Photographer of the Year.

ILLUSTRATION CREDITS

ii Dagmar Fabricius and Randy Taylor (ICS)
vi Thomas Epting
5 Robin Bowman
6 Joel Sartore
8 Rich Frishman
10 Rich Frishman
11 Rich Frishman
12 Rich Frishman
13 Rich Frishman
14 Joel Sartore
15 C. J. Walker (with digital manipulation by Impact Media Group)
16 Jan Sonnenmair
17 Barbara Ries
18 Barbara Ries
19 Barbara Ries
20 Tony McDonough
21 Tony McDonough
22 Olivier Laude
23 Olivier Laude
24 Rick Rickman
25 Rick Rickman
26 Paul Chesley
27 Ed Kashi
28 Joel Sartore
29 Vera Lentz
30 Ed Kashi
31 Ed Kashi
32 Barry Lewis
33 Barry Lewis
34 Robin Bowman
35 Robin Bowman
36 Dagmar Fabricius and Randy Taylor (ICS)
38 Paul Chesley
40 Paul Chesley
41 Paul Chesley
42 Paul Chesley
43 Paul Chesley
44 Keri Pickett
45 Keri Pickett
46 Acey Harper
47 Tim Kelly
48 Joel Sartore
49 Ed Kashi
50 Rick Rickman
51 Rick Rickman
52 Rick Rickman
53 Rick Rickman
54 top, Rich Frishman; bottom, Phil Schermeister
55 Rich Frishman
56 Phil Schermeister
57 Robert Holmes
58 Lori Grinker
59 Lori Grinker
60 Lori Grinker
61 Lori Grinker

62 Joel Sartore
64 Joel Sartore
65 Joel Sartore
66 Rick Rickman
67 Rick Rickman
68 Acey Harper
69 Acey Harper
70 top, Joel Sartore; bottom, Robert Holmes
71 Phil Schermeister
72 Acey Harper
73 Matthew Naythons
74 Joel Sartore
75 Drew Perine
77 Jonathan Olley
79 Vera Lentz
80 Joel Sartore
82 Acey Harper
83 Ed Kashi
84 Acey Harper
85 Acey Harper
86 left, Acey Harper; right, Ed Kashi
87 Mark Philbrick
88 Acey Harper
89 Acey Harper
90 top, Acey Harper; bottom, Ed Kashi
91 Acey Harper
92 Acey Harper
94 Acey Harper
95 Forest McMullin
96 Forest McMullin
97 Forest McMullin
98 Dagmar Fabricius and Randy Taylor (ICS)
99 Dagmar Fabricius and Randy Taylor (ICS)
100 Joel Sartore
101 Ed Kashi
102 Joel Sartore
103 Joel Sartore
104 Joel Sartore
105 Joel Sartore
106 Joel Sartore
107 Joel Sartore
108 Claus Meyer
110 Claus Meyer
111 Claus Meyer
112 Claus Meyer
113 Claus Meyer
114 Clockwise from top left, Nikolai Ignatiev (Network), Paul Chesley, Taro Yamasaki, Robin Bowman, Nina Barnett
115 Robin Bowman
116 Joel Sartore
117 Lori Grinker
118 top, Paul Chesley; bottom, Joel Sartore

119 C. J. Walker
120 top and bottom, Lori Grinker; middle, Robert Holmes
121 Emmanuel Santos
122 C. J. Walker
123 Joel Sartore
124 Vera Lentz
125 Vera Lentz
126 Robin Bowman
128 Taro Yamasaki
129 Taro Yamasaki
130 Kim Komenich
132 Joel Sartore
133 Taro Yamasaki
134 Taro Yamasaki
135 Lori Grinker
136 Nikolai Ignatiev (Network)
137 Joel Sartore
138 Doug Menuez
139 Doug Menuez
140 Joel Sartore
141 Joel Sartore
142 Acey Harper
143 Acey Harper
144 Joel Sartore
145 Dagmar Fabricius and Randy Taylor (ICS)
146 Mark Atkinson
147 Mark Atkinson
149 Acey Harper
150 Joel Sartore
152 Joel Sartore
153 Joel Sartore
154 Joel Sartore
155 Joel Sartore
156 C. J. Walker
157 Joel Sartore
158 Dagmar Fabricius and Randy Taylor (ICS)
159 Dagmar Fabricius and Randy Taylor (ICS)
160 Lori Grinker
161 Robin Bowman
162 Rich Frishman
163 Rich Frishman
164 Robert Holmes
165 Robert Holmes
166 Mark Atkinson

167 Mark Atkinson
168 Barry Lewis
169 Barry Lewis
170 Barry Lewis
171 Barry Lewis
172 Barry Lewis
173 Barry Lewis
174 Nikolai Ignatiev (Network)
176 Nikolai Ignatiev (Network)
177 Nikolai Ignatiev (Network)
178 Nikolai Ignatiev (Network)
179 Nikolai Ignatiev (Network)
180 Joel Sartore
181 Joel Sartore
182 Acey Harper
183 Acey Harper
184 Acey Harper
185 Acey Harper
186 Paul Chesley
187 Ed Kashi
188 Gideon Mendel
189 Tomasz Tomaszewski
190 Acey Harper
191 Nina Barnett
192 Joel Sartore
193 Joel Sartore
194 top, Joel Sartore, bottom, Paul Chesley
195 Lori Grinker
196 Acey Harper
197 Acey Harper
198 Emmanuel Santos
199 Emmanuel Santos
200 Doug Menuez
201 Doug Menuez
202 Ed Kashi
203 Ed Kashi
204 Robin Bowman
205 Robin Bowman
206 Torin Boyd
207 Torin Boyd
208 Lori Grinker
209 Lori Grinker
211 Acey Harper
213 Robin Bowman
214 Robin Bowman
226 Keith Dannemiller

Digital photo manipulation by IMPACT MEDIA GROUP
Based in San Francisco, the Impact Media Group was founded in 1992 by artists Garner Moss, Greg Munson, and Trey Roski, and specializes in digitally altering photographic images.

E-6 photo processing by THE NEW LAB
Founded in 1981 by Sam Hoffman and Arsenio Lopez, the San Francisco–based New Lab provides high-quality photo processing and customer service to the professional photographic community.

ACKNOWLEDGMENTS

Epicenter Communications and Warner Books would like to express their appreciation to the First Presidency of The Church of Jesus Christ of Latter-day Saints, the Quorum of the Twelve Apostles, and the staff of the Church Public Affairs Department for their cooperation in making this book possible.

Patrons

Alan and Karen Ashton
Joseph and Janeal Cannon
Dana and Chris Doggett
Keith and Anna Halls
Steven and Kalleen Lund
Blake and Nancy Roney

Advisors and Friends

Oscar Aguayo
Dave Albrecht
Bill Allen
John & Rebecca Altberg
Luis Alvarez
Dan Andersen
Howard Andersen, Jr.
Heidi K. Anderson
LaMont Anderson
Nona Anderson
Kirk Anspach
Denise Antoine
Burt & David Arnowitz
James Arpe
Keith Atkinson
Sam Atoa
Arnold R. Augustin
Richard M. Austin
Laurel D. Bailey
Alan Baker
Nancy L. Baker
Clive Barney
Peter Barr
George S. Barrus
Noel Barton
Milton Batalion
Lavar & Helen Bateman
Jeffrey Bateson
Andy Bechtolsheim
Ken Beck
Ray E. Beckham
Paul H. Beckstrand
Carol D. Bee
Pamela Bellwood
Gustavo Berasaluce
Michel Bernard
George & Keetje Berndt
Howard Biddulph

Dale K. Bills
John Blair
Robert Blair
Gene Blumberg
The Lee Bodily family
Lucas Bonnier
Boy's Life
Jessica Brackman
Rebecca Brackman
Richard Bretzing
Hoyt W. Brewster, Jr.
Leora S. Brockbank
Harold C. Brown
S. Kent Brown
Gary Browning
Philip Bryson
Hart Bullock
David & Iris Burnett
Dr. Stanley & Sara Burns
Jim Burton
Jerry P. Cahill
Mark Call
Berverly Campbell
Ann L. Cannaday
Lindy Carlson
Lynn Carson
Dr. Frank Catchpool
Anthony Catsimatides
Ray Cave
Centers for Disease
   Control
Gina & Mike Cerre
Howard Chapnick
Richard Chapple
Boyd Christensen
Carol Christensen
Jean Christensen
Lorna Christianson

Paul K. Clark
Ron Clark
Richard Clarke
Mike Clary
Dr. Harris Clearfield
Ray Close
John G. Cobbs
David Cohen
Jennifer Coley
Michael Patrick Collins
Jimmy Colton
Patte Comstock
John Connolly
Contact Press Images
Joy Conwell
Tolli Cooper
Coral Graphics
Troy Lee Corriveau
Paul Alan Cox
Scott R. Crapo
Carl & Tina Crathorne
Graeme Cray
Sherm M. Crump
John M. Cyrocki
Tom Daniels
Michael Dashe
Leon A. Davies
Marilyn W. Davies
Yvonne Davis
Mike Davis
Sashka T. Dawg
Dr. Arthur Deikman
Ray DeMoullin
Marty Derrick
Kent Derricott
Sandro Diani
Al Diaz
Marco Diaz de Leon

Robert P. DeVecchi
Elaine Doxey
Joanne Doxey
Sam Doxey
Larry W. Draper
Arnold & Elaine Drapkin
Rich D'Souza
Noel Duerden
Valena Duvall
Dana Dyer
Eastman Kodak Company
Val N. Edwards
Maureen Mahon & David
   Egen
Gloria Emerson
Richard Emery
Eugene England
Noel H. Enniss
Dale Ensign
Alan Erickson
The William S. & Gloria
   Evans Family
Dr. Timothy S. Evans
Matt Evans
Karl Farnsworth
Fathom Pictures
Faulkner Color Labs
Ike Ferguson
Peter Ferguson
David Fewster
Val Fisher
Robert S. Fotheringham
FPG International
Ronald G. Francis
Eleanor Naythons
   Freedman
Frank Freeman
David Friend
Joseph Fritzner
Joshua & Selena Fuller
Roger T. Fuller
Parley K. Fullmer
Jamie Gangell
Rebecca Gardner
Joseph Garfield
Ricardo Gaya
Geneva Steel
Levon Gifford
Gurcharan Singh Gill
Wendy Gimbel
Global Village
Kate Godfrey
Mark Godfrey
Heber Geurtz
Mary-Margaret Goggin
Kathy Golden
Ray & Claire Golden
Walter Gonzales

Todd K. Goulding
David Gourley
Bryan J. Grant
Graphics Resource
Michaelene Grassi
Don Grayston
Carol Gray
Mel Griffith
John Grinceri
Sister Grob
Dr. Mary Ellen Guroy
The John & Connie
   Gustafson Family
Don & Kristin Guy
Bruce Haight
Janette C. Hales
Troy Hall
Anne Hamilton
Evelyn O. Hammond
John E. Hardy
Gary & Ann Hare
Brent Harker
Reed & Doris Harker
Cindy R. Harper
April Star Harper
Norman Harris
Connie Haruch
Craig R. Haslam
Brian Hatch
Verian Hawkins
Ray Hendershot
Matthew & Jeannine
   Herron
Lloyd Hess
Harriet Heyman
Allyson Hill
Sterling Hill
Doug Hind
Dr. Harry & Sharon
   Hirsch
Clark E. Hirschi
Sam Hoffman
Brent Holiday
Bill Homer
John & Barbara Homer
Kim Honda
Daniel Horne
Dave Horne
David Howells
Craig Hunt
Mark Hurst
Darlene Hutchison
Ryuichi Inoue
International Center of
   Photography
Grant R. Ipsen
It's CD
Elaine L. Jack

Fred & Barbara Jacobs
Pearl & Arnold Jacobs
Peter Jaret
John Jeffrey
Paul Jensen
Steven H. Jensen
Don Jesse
Ed Johnson
Jeffrey Johnson
Jennie B. Johnson
James Johnston
Bill & Sarah Joy
Phil & Dora Judson
Just Film
Del Justiniano
Davyani Kamdar
Patricia Keim
Robb Kendrick
Jim Kelly
David & Rebecca
    Kennerly
Jim Kerl
Bonnie King
S. Nick King
Roy H. King
Jerry Kirk
Doug & Francoise
    Kirkland
Laurence J. Kirshbaum
Emmanuel Kissi
Jo Ann Klundt
Keith Klundt
Paul E. Koelliker
Gene Korr
James Kozlik
Virgil Kovalenko
Harvey-Jane Kowal
Janet Kruckenberg
Eliane & J. P. Laffont
Linda Lamb
Rupta & Vishuas Lambley
Clive Langley
Mary Lapegna
Jim Larsen
Elder & Sister Leeuwen
L. Don LeFevre
The Paul L. & Janice W.
    Legler family
Michael Leonard
Glen Leonard
Carla Levdar
Rebecca R. Levin
Dr. Carl & Karen Levitsky
Larry Levitsky
Liaison Photopress
    Agency
Life
Jerel Lindley

Allen Litster
Joe Livingston
Jeanne M. Lloyd
Arsenio Lopez
David Lowe
Jaime Marques Lucher
Peter Macchia
Dr. Robert & Bernadette
    Mack
Ann Madsen
Truman Madsen
Magnum Photos
John & Leslie Markoff
David Markus
Dr. James Mason
Jim Matheson
Roger L. Matkin
Julia Mavimbela
Kitty McCallum
J. L. McCrary
Hiriam McDonald
Liz McGrath
Arthur McKinlay
Keith B. McMullin
Arden McQueen
Charlotte "Arkie" Meisner
Juan Mencia
Dorothy Mendolson
Stan Menscher
Tereza Menuez
Craig Merrell
Derek F. Metcalfe
Keith & Lori Metzger
Gill Meyer
Stanley Michelsen
Peter Miller
Ronald A. Millett
Charles E. Mitchener
Modern Effects
Phillip Moffitt
Sherrie Moore
Kenneth Morasethla
Pauline Morello
Michael Moritz
John R. Morrey
Loren Morris
Wayne Morris
Charles Muldowney
Ignosi Naga
National Geographic
Benjamin & Bill Naythons
Mattie Eleanor Naythons
Susan Walker Naythons
William T. Naythons
Nanscy Neiman
Arlo Nelson
Evan Nelson
Glade Nelson

Clayton C. Newell
Newsweek
Bonnie Nielson
Nikon Professional
    Services
Rod & Sheila Nordland
Steve Novakavich
Chicko Okazaki
Daniel Okrent
Bruce L. & Christine
    Olsen
Christine A. Olson
Jeff Orr
Keith L. Orr
Dan Oshima
Elder Ostvig
Michael R. Otterson
Lloyd Owen
Rafael Ozumo
Lynn J. Packham
Holly Palance
Jill Palmer
C. Gerald Parker
Edward Partridge
Dennis Peart
Cecile Pelous
Pedro Penha
Jim Perry
Brent Petersen
Stanley Peterson
Robert Pledge
Robert Poll
Gerald L. Pond
Leland & Kit Poole
Kayla Porter
Elisa Pulido
Dr. Robert & P. A. Rabkin
Richard Rabkin
Carolyn Rasmus
Malcom Rea
Refugees International
Stuart C. Reid
Reportáge Stock
Tom Rielly
Bonner Ritchie
Maureen Roberts
Thomas Rogers
Steve Ross
Jeffrey Roundy
Roy Rowan
Galen & Barbara Rowell
Elder Rudd
George Russ
Donald G. Russell
Doug Rytting
Marcel Saba
Saba Press Agency
Barbara Sadick

Ellen Aree Sanok
William Sarnoff
Wolfgang Schmullius
William Scoville
Bobby & Patty Seidman
Keith Sellers
Ruth Shapiro
Carol, Michael, and
    Rosalie Sheggeby
Ron Shelton
Jerald Sherwood
Aaron Schindler
Kristina Schreck
Dale R. Shumway
Ed Siady
Susan Siegel
Bill Silcock
Goksun Sipahioglu
Gabriele Sirtl
Vladimir Siwachok
Leif & Ann Skoogfors
William W. Slaughter
T. LaMar Sleight
William B. Smart
Boyd Smith
Stanley & Mary Ellen
    Smoot
David E. Sorensen
John Sorensen
Roger Spottiswoode
Damar Stanicia
Carol Steed
Brent Steenblik
Michele Stephenson
Arthur Stout
Barry Sundermeier
SuperMac Technology
Michele Susoev
Claron Swenson
Swen Swenson
Paul Taggart
Arthur & Kathryn Taylor
Rebecca Taylor
James Tew
F. Weldon Thacker
Gordon Thatcher
John Thomas
Kirk Thomas
Joan E. Thompson
Norm Thompson
Judith Thurman
Time
Barbara Timothy
Lini To'o
Jay Todd
Larry Topham
David O. Trevino
Wendy Truslove

Tim Tucker
Richard Turley, Jr.
Merlene J. Turner
Mark N. Tuttle
Samisoni Uasila'a
U.S. News & World Report
Bill Valor
C.I. Rex Van Coller
Dell R. Van Orden
Jacques & Larry Vidal
Michael von Rosen Jr.
Alan Wakeley
Walter Walker
Jimmy Walker
J. Don Wardle
Tom Whatley
Janet C. Watson
Elder Wentz
Nick Wheeler
Blaine Whipple
Charles White
J. T. Whitworth
Dianne Wildman
Preston & Dotty Williams
Ray Williamson
Curtis P. Wilson
Jared Winburn
Chuck Wing
Jeff & Catherine Wise
Robin Wolaner
Howard Wolfgraham
Steve Young
Patrick Zerbib
Jerry Zimmerman

ALL TRANSPARENCY FILM PROCESSED BY
THE NEW LAB AND A&I COLOR LABS.
BLACK-AND-WHITE PHOTOGRAPHIC
PROCESSING AND PRINTING BY
KIRK ANSPACH AT GRAPHICS RESOURCE.
COLOR PROCESSING AND PRINTING BY
LIGHT WAVES AND FAULKNER COLOR LABS.
SLIDE DUPLICATION BY
MODERN EFFECTS.
TYPESET IN MINION AND CENTAUR.
PRINTED AND BOUND BY
AMILCARE PIZZI, MILAN.

Above: Dedication of the 2,000th stake in Mexico City.
Photograph: Keith Dannemiller